THINKING BEANS

A YEAR OF CLASSROOM PHIL(

by David Birch

one
slice
books

Published by:

The Philosophyman Ltd

7 Tower Road, Writtle

 Chelmsford, CM1 3NR, UK

Email: jason@thephilosophyman.com

Web: www.thephilosophyman.com

Tel: +44 (0) 1245 830123

Design by Kerim Hudson, Illustrations by Andrea Rošková.

ABOUT THE AUTHOR

David Birch teaches philosophy and religious studies at Highgate School in London. He also works with the Philosophy Foundation, an educational charity that takes philosophy into schools, workplaces and the wider community. He is the author of *Provocations: Philosophy for Secondary School*

ACKNOWLEDGMENTS

Many of the lessons in this book grew out of my philosophy classes at the hospital school in Great Ormond Street Hospital. I am thankful to the wonderful children I met there over the years and to the dedicated staff, including Jubeda Begum, Susy Griffiths, Ziva O'Connor-Hanlon and Danielle Valdar. My thanks also to Emma Worley at the Philosophy Foundation for plonking me there in the first place.

I also wish to thank the strange creatures in my 19/20 year 7 classes and the Philosophy Club regulars at Kensington Park School, as well as the many boys I taught at St Anthony's in Hampstead, whose thoughts and ideas have helped shape this book.

And I am grateful to Jason Buckley for enabling the book to see the light of day.

'What shall I learn of beans or beans of me?'

Henry David Thoreau, *Walden*

CONTENTS

INTRODUCTION

This is a book of beans. When sown among your class they will produce roots and shoots and tendrils of thought. If a pocket of time opens up in your day, pick it up, flip it open and start a philosophical discussion. It can accommodate a variety of needs, with the lessons expanding or contracting at will. Many of them could easily consume an hour, and all of them can be chopped up and squeezed into 15 minutes.

To help you get germinating, we'll start by running through some basic tips and suggestions on how to sustain a philosophical conversation with your class.

Though sometimes embroidered with jargon and initialisms, a confabulatory approach to teaching philosophy is actually quite simple. Since your aim is to elicit rather than impart, your role is more passive than active (the students' activity is enabled by the teacher's passivity, they wax as you wane). Like an efficient piece of technology, you should become more or less unnoticed.

Here, in summary, is a suggested approach:

1. Ask the main question.

2. Give students 30 seconds to discuss it with the person next to them before starting a group discussion – this is an opportunity for them to find their thoughts and use their voices.

3. Ask for a show of hands for those who think 'Yes', 'No', 'Not sure' or 'Something else' – this is an aperitif to the discussion. It helps to make all students feel involved and invested as well as allowing them to see the range of views within the classroom. This often creates the desire to know why others are thinking differently.

4. Take contributions and sometimes follow these up by asking

the students why they think what they do. By asking 'Why?' you are encouraging the students to explore the intricacies and potential of their thoughts; you're allowing their thoughts to grow.

5. Try to foster dialogues and responses among the students. If you notice that a particular contribution is exciting a lot of interest, this is a good opportunity to encourage dialogue by asking whether anyone has a response to that point.

You can, in short, have an entirely effective session by following a basic pattern of *What, Why, Next*: 'What do you think?', 'Why do you think it?', move on to the next student.

Here are a few Dos and Don'ts:

> — Do say: *'Are you saying such-and-such?'*
> Don't say: *'So you're saying such-and-such.'*

Before you prompt the student to think more deeply about her answer, it's worthwhile simply repeating it, partly so you can check you've heard it correctly and partly because it gives the class another chance to hear the idea. But avoid phrasing this as 'So you're saying...' Using a question rather than a declarative gives the student a clearer opportunity to either change her mind or reject your wording (though we should always endeavour to use the student's wording, it is easy to slip into our own idiolect).

> — Do say: *'Why do you think that?'*
> Don't say: *'Can you explain that?'*

The aim of asking 'Why?' is not make the student justify or elucidate her answer but to explore it further. You are inviting her to think beyond her thought, yet asking for explanations can sound demanding rather than inviting. Indeed, asking 'Why?' can in itself sound like a demand, so you might alternatively ask, 'Can you say more about that?'

— Do say: *'Are you talking about the soul?'*
Don't say: *'You're talking about the soul.'*

Sometimes you might notice that in their answers students seem to be circling round a particular concept without quite landing on it. It can be useful to introduce this concept into the discussion since it can serve as a catalyst or a bridge in their thinking. However, you want to avoid imposing the concept on them – it might have nothing to do with what they were thinking and may be entirely unhelpful. This is why you should present the concept to them in the form of a question, thereby affording them the opportunity to take it or leave it.

— Do say: *'Can you say more about that?'*
Don't say: *'What an excellent idea!'*

It's best to refrain from praising contributions. We tend to believe that we ought to praise students in order to encourage them. However, simply being listened to is often enough. Praising contributions also implies that there are norms by which they are being judged. This is potentially inhibiting. If you are praising you are not thinking, and you want to show the student that their ideas are not final and understood but open, absorbing and catalytic.

Rather than assuming the stance of a benevolent judge, your role is to model a kind of idiocy or bafflement. To this end, you must be willing to bid farewell to your dignity. I have overheard children speculating that I never went to school and have no GCSEs. One 6-year-old delightedly exclaimed, 'You're like a child! You don't know anything!'

By asking questions and exhibiting confusion, you are showing that philosophy is a subject that renders one's education redundant, that to find the answer you have to think for yourself. The abdication of your epistemic authority provides students with a space in which they can think and explore for themselves. Within the context of a philosophy session, you should suspend your own beliefs and opinions and become empty-headed, a cauldron of curiosity.

In terms of troubleshooting, students sometimes offer contributions of which you cannot see the relevance. When this happens, instead of trying to interpret their comments, simply repeat the question. Repeating the question is also useful for students when they get muddled and forget what they meant to say. Hearing the question again often helps to focus their thoughts and regain their bearings.

The extent to which you keep the discussion focused on the main questions or let it digress and meander is up to you. I don't know whether there is any particular virtue in keeping the discussion oriented around certain questions beyond the fact that within a larger class it ensures the discussion is easy to follow. But with a group of, say, up to 12, you can often let the discussion go all over the place without leaving anyone behind.

Beneath some of the main questions I have included subsidiary questions. These lay out the philosophical terrain of the main question and show the various strands of possible development. They are optional follow-ups that you may wish to pose in order to challenge your students further. I tend to keep them on ice for the first few contributions and if the discussion doesn't seem to be evolving in any interesting way and I'm noticing repetition among the answers, I use follow-up questions to give the discussion a new spin and freshen it up. This helps to elicit some new thoughts while showing the class the multifaceted complexities of the initial question.

Since the lessons are not driving towards any particular insight or piece of knowledge, you can, as mentioned above, modify them at will. You might have a 10-minute discussion only asking one question from a given session or a whole hour exploring every detail. Feel free to customise and experiment.

If you do wish to include a kind of plenary, though conclusions are somewhat antithetical to the spirit of beans, you can end with a brief segment of 'Maybe conclusions': 'In conclusion, then, maybe...' and here you take several contributions from students on their closing thoughts.

Finally, if you happen to have a class of students who are reticent or reluctant to enter into a discussion because they are averse to argument, reassure them that disagreements and differences needn't be adversarial. The project of a philosophy lesson can be viewed as collaborative. The aim is to develop and discover as many different thoughts and ideas as possible. You are seeking an abundance of ideas, not a single definitive one. And where ideas do clash and collide the results are often generative; their frictional energy can lead to a host of new ideas, which themselves may clash and collide, and on it goes.

BRAINS

Topic According to the American philosopher Thomas Nagel you weigh approximately 1.4 kg. This is because you weigh as much as your brain (your other bits are irrelevant). In fact, it makes no sense to speak of the weight of your brain because you don't have a brain – you are one. Animalism, on the other hand, is a theory which claims we are not *parts* (brains, say) of animals, rather, we *are* animals.

This lesson uses a brain transplant scenario to explore what we are and, incidentally, how much we weigh.

Props Two different looking hats and a stuffed animal

Action **1** Ask two volunteers of the same sex to sit down on parallel chairs facing the class. Place the two hats on their heads. These represent their respective brains. Explain to the class that you are going to perform a brain transplant i.e. you're going to swap their hats. (To add a little colour, use a pen as an imaginary hacksaw and produce anatomically vile sound effects, squelches and whatnot.)

With the operation complete, refer to one of the volunteers (*x*) and ask –

– *Question* **1a** Where is *x* now?

  – Where is *x*'s personality?
  – Where are *x*'s memories?
  – Where is *x*'s smile?
  – Does *x* have a new body or a new brain?

— *Question* **1b** Who should *x*'s parents take home after school?

    — Which person did *x*'s parents drop off this morning?
    — Which person did *x*'s mother give birth to?

Action **2** Perform the same operation but using students of different sexes. Referring to one of the volunteers (*x*) –

— *Question* **2** Is *x* now a girl/ boy?

Action **3** Perform the same action but using one student and a stuffed animal (a soft flamingo, for instance).

— *Question* **3** Is *x* now a flamingo?

    — Is *x* a human in a flamingo's body or an actual flamingo?
    — Is this one animal two different species?

Action **4** Finally, place *x*'s hat on a chair by itself and ask the class to imagine that it is kept 'alive' by having a machine pump blood through its veins and arteries.

— *Question* **4** Is this *x*?

    — Is this a human?
    — Does it have a sex?
    — If I've never seen *x*'s brain, does that mean I've never seen *x*?

This final scenario isn't mere science fiction: scientists at Yale University have performed a similar feat with the brains of pigs. Now, to bring the fundamental philosophical distinction to the fore, you could write on the board, 'I am a brain' and 'I have a brain', and ask the class which statement is correct.

HANDS & FACES

Topic Like **BRAINS**, this lesson involves transplantation, but our concern here is with questions of possession rather than identity.

Props Two pairs of different looking gloves and two different looking masks

Action **1** Ask two volunteers (*x* and *y*) to sit on parallel chairs facing the class and tell them to put the gloves on (these represent their hands.) Now ask the class to imagine that during the night a mischievous surgeon snuck into their bedrooms, surgically removed the hands of each volunteer and attached them to the other. Swap the volunteers' gloves to illustrate this (sound effects encouraged).

With the operation complete, point to one of the volunteer's (*x*) hands and ask –

    – *Question* **1** Are these *x*'s hands?

       – If they are not *x*'s, when she uses them to touch her nose, is it *y* touching her nose?
       – If they are not *x*'s, when the hands feel cold, is she feeling a sensation that is not in her body?
       – If they are not *x*'s, and if only one hand from each person were swapped, when *x* held the two hands together, would she be holding hands with *y*?
       – If they are now *x*'s, does *y* have no right to ask for them back?
       – If they are now *x*'s and they have a scar from where *y* previously burnt them, does that mean that *y* scarred *x*'s hands?
       – If it's a matter of time, how long would it

take for them to become *x*'s hands?

Action **2** Ask for another two volunteers (*x* and *y*). Describe the same scenario and perform the same operation, except this time with masks and faces rather than gloves and hands. This is to test whether the answers from the previous question change depending on the body part.

Though the images are quite graphic, you can prime your class for this discussion by showing them before-and-after pictures of actual face transplants.

Pointing to *x*, ask –

— *Question* **2** Is this *x*'s face?

   — When *x* looks in the mirror, who does she see?
   — If it's a matter of time, how long would
     it take for it to become *x*'s face?
   — If it is not *x*'s, when she licks the lips, is she licking *y*'s lips?
   — If it is not *x*'s, when she puts eyeshadow on, is
     she not putting eyeshadow on herself?

VOICES

Topic The voice is not without its paradoxes. Though part of us, it seems to only exist in its departure from us: unless I speak I have no voice, but as soon as I have spoken my voice is gone. It is that piece of ourselves we possess only in its vanishing. And it is that piece of ourselves that can only exist beyond us. It thus dissolves the boundaries between ourselves and the world. And though our bodies may be dwarfed by caverns and halls, our voices can fill them; unlike the body, the voice can expand and shrink at will, from a bellow to a whisper. It carries our thoughts and promises and yet is a substance no firmer than air.

Props None

Action **1** In unison ask the class to repeat a certain word five times, 'conker' for instance. Then ask them to sit in silence for 5 seconds.

> — *Question* **1** Does your voice still exist while you are silent?
>
>> — If it does still exist, where is it?
>> — Does it make sense to say that we have a silent voice?
>> — Is your voice an ability or an entity?
>> — If it does not exist, do you have a different voice every time you speak?

Action **2** OK, this is pretty weird, nevertheless… ask the class to sit with their mouths open while a volunteer (*x*) loudly says a word, 'gargoyle' for instance.

> — *Question* **2** Did *x*'s voice enter your mouth?

- If *x*'s voice entered your ears, does that
  mean it also entered your mouth?
- If you swallow while *x* is talking, are
  you swallowing her voice?
- If *x*'s voice entered your mouth, does that
  mean her words entered it too?

Action 3 Ask a volunteer (*x*) to loudly say a word, 'defenestrate' for instance. Ask another (*y*) to stand at the back of the room, and another (*z*) to stand midway between the other two.

  — *Question* 3 Who is closest to *x*'s voice?

- Is being close to the source of the voice the
  same as being close to the voice?
- If *x*'s voice exists everywhere it can be heard, is
  everyone who hears it the same distance from it?
- If *x*'s voice exists everywhere it can be heard, is there
  any distance between it and those who can hear it?
- Is it possible to get closer to *x*'s voice than *x* is?
- Where is *x*'s voice?

Action 4 Ask the class to imagine a man standing beside a jet engine screaming as loudly as he can. His aim is to try to hear his own voice, but so great is the din he can only hear the sound of the engine.

  — *Question* 4 Is the man making a sound?

- If the man is impossible to hear, is he silent?
- If a sound is impossible to hear, does it exist?
- If he isn't making a sound, is he even screaming?

Action **5** Show the class this argument –

Your voice is a large part of who you are, and your voice is made of air, so you are largely made of air.

    – *Question* **5** Is this correct?

        – If your voice is a part of you, and your voice travels at 343 metres per second (the speed of sound), does that mean you can travel at 343 metres per second?

THOUGHTS

Topic The French philosopher René Descartes was puzzled by the question of what he essentially was, but he eventually came to the conclusion that he was a thinking thing. And though he was satisfied with this answer, arguably all he had done was taken one mystery and replaced it with another, namely, the mystery of what thinking is (this is referred to as obscurum per obscurius – explaining the obscure through the more obscure). He may well be a thinking thing, but unless we know what thinking is, how much does this really tell us?

In terms of the location of thoughts, while it may seem natural to say that thoughts are in the brain, the ancient Greek Zeno of Citium argued that since the voice carries thought, thoughts must come from the same place as the voice. And latterly, the English philosopher Peter Hacker has argued that we shouldn't regard thought as residing in any part of us. Thinking is something that people do, not their parts. Though brains may be necessary for thinking, it doesn't follow that thoughts are in the brain. Analogously, though jet engines are necessary for flight, it makes no sense to say that flight is in the engines.

Props None

Action **1** Tell the class they are going to run a few thinking experiments. To start with, ask them to shake their heads.

— *Question* **1** When you shake your head are you shaking your thoughts too?

- — Are thoughts inside your head?
- — Do thoughts have a location?
- — Can thoughts move?
- — Can you feel them in any particular place?

— If your thoughts are inside your head,
  are your desires there too?

Action **2** If you happen not to be blessed with acrobatic students, ask the class to simply imagine doing a handstand while thinking about something, anything – strawberries, for instance.

— *Question* **2** When you are upside down, are your thoughts upside down too?

  — Do sleeping bats have upside down dreams?

Action **3** Divide the class in two: ask one half to think about a very large elephant and the other a very tiny mouse.

— *Question* **3** Are the thoughts of the elephant half larger than the thoughts of the mouse half?

  — Do thoughts have size?
  — Do thoughts occupy space?
  — Do elephants have larger thoughts than mice?

Action **4** Ask the class to close their eyes and think of a clear blue sky.

— *Question* **4** When you think of the sky are your thoughts blue?

  — When you think of the clear blue sky,
    are you experiencing blue?
  — If the thought isn't blue, then how do we know
    that we are not thinking of a red sky?
  — What is the difference between thinking of
    a blue sky and thinking of a red sky?
  — If thoughts can have colour, can they have smells too?

Action **5** Brace yourself for a cacophony: ask the class collectively to try to speak faster than they can think.

— *Question* **5** Can you speak faster than you can think?

— Can we act without thinking?
— Is talking a kind of thinking?

Action **6** Finally, ask the class to think of anything they wish and then try to focus very carefully on the thought to see what it is made of. Give them a few moments.

— *Question* **6** Are thoughts made of anything?

— Do thoughts have parts?
— Are thoughts made of words?
— Are thoughts things like eyeballs or actions like looking?
— Are thoughts physical?
— Do thoughts have weight?
— If they are not made of anything, do they even exist?
— Is being made of nothing the same as being nothing?

INTERACTION

Topic This session considers the possibilities of interaction. Through acts of holding, touching, consuming and licking, it explores how and whether we can interact with colour, beauty, the universe, life and each other.

To arbitrarily pluck one pertinent view, here's the Portuguese writer Fernando Pessoa from *The Book of Disquiet*: 'When we grasp an attractive body, it's not beauty but fatty and cellular flesh that we embrace; our kiss doesn't touch the mouth's beauty but the wet flesh of decaying, membranous lips...'

To pluck another, here's John Locke: 'light, heat, whiteness, or coldness, are no more really in [fire and snow] than sickness or pain is in manna. Take away the sensation of them; let not the eyes see light or colours, nor the ears hear sounds; let the palate not taste, nor the nose smell; and all colours, tastes, odours, and sounds, as they are such particular ideas, vanish and cease...'

Props One cherry and something beautiful

Action **1** Ask a volunteer to eat a cherry.

> — *Question* **1** *x* ate a cherry. Did she also eat its redness?
>> — If yes: is she now digesting its redness?
>> — If no: where did the redness go?
>> — Is redness *in* the cherry?
>> — Can colours be chewed?
>> — Did she also eat its shape?

Action **2** Show the class something beautiful (a flower or a stone, say). Go round and ask a few students to touch it.

> — *Question* **2** When you touch a beautiful thing, are you touching its beauty?
>
>> — If you can destroy beauty with your hands,
>>   does that mean that you can touch it too?
>> — If beauty can be touched, does it have a distinctive feel?
>> — Is beauty *in* the object?

Action **3** If you happen to have class pets, this would be an excellent opportunity to afford them the limelight. Otherwise ask for two volunteers, preferably one strong and the other light, and instruct one to lift the other up.

> — *Question* **3** When you hold a living thing, are you holding its life?
>
>> — Is your life *in* your body?
>> — Does your life exist entirely in the present?
>> — If life can be ended with one's hands, does that
>>   mean it can be touched with them too?
>> — When you look at a living tree, are you looking
>>   at its life? What does its life look like?
>> — When you take a photograph of a living
>>   tree, is its life in the photograph?

Action **4** Ask the class to lick their lips.

> — *Question* **4** When you lick your lips, are you licking the universe?
>
>> — Are your lips part of the universe?
>> — If you lick part of something, are you
>>   thereby licking that thing?

— If no, then what do you have to do to lick the universe?

Action **5** Open a book at a random page and ask a volunteer to smell it.

— *Question* **5** Are you smelling words?

- If you smell the page, and the words are on the page, are you smelling words?
- If words can be seen, can they also be smelt?
- Does the same word printed in different books – given that it is the same word – have the same smell?
- Would two people who smell the different books be smelling the same thing?
- Are words physical things?
- Do all physical things have smells?
- If you spelt out the word 'cheese' using oregano, would it be right to say that 'cheese' smells of oregano?
- How many words can you smell in a single sniff?

To go for a wander, you could look at that strange moment in the Book of Ezekiel where God instructs Ezekiel to eat a scroll on which were written 'words of lament and mourning and woe'. Ezekiel dutifully obeys and finds that the scroll tastes of honey. It's not clear why he was asked to do this – did God think that by consuming the scroll he'd assimilate its contents? Is this a more intimate and direct form of reading? For our purposes it raises the following question: by eating the scroll, was Ezekiel eating its words?

(Curiously, this is not the only allusion to word consumption by a Jewish prophet. In the Book of Jeremiah the eponymous prophet speaks of eating God's words. Though he doesn't specify how he did this, he does describe it as a most fulfilling experience.)

Action 6 Ask the class to turn to the person next to them and pat them on the back.

— *Question* 6 Were you touching the person or were you only touching their clothes?

- If they can feel you, does that mean
  they are being touched by you?
- If two people are holding hands while wearing gloves, are
  they actually holding hands or are they only holding gloves?

OBJECTS

Topic In relation to ourselves the question of objecthood has received considerable philosophical attention. Immanuel Kant, for instance, argued that we should not use or exploit others since our ability to think and act for ourselves elevates us above the status of objects.

In relation to one's body, the French philosopher Maurice Merleau-Ponty argued that it is not an 'object of the world' but 'our general medium for having a world'. That is to say, whereas objects are that which we can handle and examine, the body is that through which we are able to handle and examine. Indeed, items cease being objects once they cease being things in the world and instead become things through which we interact with the world; a blind person's stick, for instance, is not an object for that person.

In relation to other questions, some philosophers have felt compelled to argue that in addition to physical objects, such as pumpkins, there exist 'abstract objects', such as numbers. The broader question, however, of whether shadows and clouds and whatnot constitute objects has received less attention. But as you'll find with this session, these are questions ripe with confusion.

Props None

Action Simply present each one of these things to the class in any order and in any way that you wish, and ask –

Words	Shadows	Sky
Burps	Clouds	Universe
Rivers	Fire	
Dreams	Fingers	
Smells	Ewes	
Kisses	You	

— *Question* Is this an object?

- — Can it be used? If so, does that make it an object?
- — Can it be owned? If so, does that make it an object?
- — Can it be held? If so, does that make it an object?
- — Does it have boundaries, a place where it ends? If not, does that mean it is not an object?
- — Does it occupy space? If not, does that mean it is not an object?
- — If it's not an object, what is it?
- — Is it made of objects?
- — If something is made of objects, does that mean it must also be an object?

SPACE

Topic The French philosopher Henri Bergson believed that we cannot see absences. When we look at an empty classroom we may say, 'There are no children here', but we do not *see* the absence of children: we see the carpet and chairs and so on, and then we make a judgment about the absence of children. However, a fellow Frenchman, Jean-Paul Sartre, disagreed and claimed that absences can be seen. When we exclaim 'There are no children here!' we perceive the absence of children, and this is an experience, not a judgment.

Yet, in outlining these ideas before a lesson on space I am presuming that space is an absence. But is it? Isaac Newton, for one, believed that space is not the absence of things but itself a particular type of thing, a sort of substance.

Props None

Action Ask the class to sit in a circle.

— *Question* **1** Can you see the space in the middle of the circle?

- — Can you describe what it looks like?
- — Does it have colour?
- — How large is it?
- — Is space invisible?
- — If you cannot see space, how do you know it is there?
- — Can space be experienced through any of your senses?

— *Question* **2** Does the space in the middle of the circle exist?

- — Is it made of anything?

— If it is *made* of nothing, does that mean it *is* nothing?
— Is space something or nothing?
— Is nothing something?
— If space is nothing, does that mean that
  you and I are separated by nothing?

DARKNESS

Topic If we think of darkness as the absence of light, then the ideas of Bergson of Sartre outlined in **SPACE** are relevant here also. But again, is darkness the absence of light or the presence of something else, of some strange sort of substance?

Props A scarf

Action **1** Tie the scarf over the volunteer's closed eyes. Ask her what she can see.

— *Question* **1** Can you see darkness?

- — Is it possible to see darkness?
- — Is darkness a substance?
- — Is darkness something or nothing?
- — Is darkness a presence or an absence?
- — Is seeing nothing the same as not seeing anything?
- — Does darkness have colour?
- — Does darkness have shape?
- — Do people with better vision see the dark more clearly?
- — If you cannot see darkness, can you not see blackness either?
- — Is darkness invisible?

To explore this question's audio equivalent, you can ask whether it is possible to hear silence. This is harder to approach experimentally, especially in a school, but you can ask the class to approach the question by imagining the cosmic silence of space (pictured within a starless void, this can actually be used to unify both the audio and visual considerations: is this suspension in blank vacuity, this total silence and encircling darkness, a sensory experience?)

Action **2** Ask everyone in the class to cup their hands together to create a sort of dark hollow, leaving an opening at the top so they can look into it. (Rather than blindfolding each student, you can also use this activity as a way for everyone in the class to explore Question 1– of course, they could also just close their eyes and cover them with their hands).

   — *Question* **2** Did you just create darkness?

- If you did, what is the darkness made out of?
- When you turn off a light or snuff out a candle, are you destroying something or creating something?
- If a god created the universe and everything in existence, did it thereby create darkness?
- Did darkness pre-exist the universe?
- Did you all create the same thing or different things?
- Is there now something in the universe that wasn't there before?
- If darkness is a nothing, did you just create a nothing?
- Did someone with larger hands create more than someone with smaller hands?

To explore the fourth subsidiary question, you could consider those cryptic lines from the ancient Hindu text *The Rig Veda* which state that before the universe 'there was neither non-existence nor existence'.

As a literary digression, you could look at John Milton's description of hell in *Paradise Lost* where he says that the infernal flames produce 'No light, but rather darkness visible'. Does this description make sense? Does it make sense to speak of radiant darkness? Though black holes suck light in, could there be a thing that spewed darkness out?

To explore the fourth subsidiary question, you could consider those cryptic lines from the ancient Hindu text *The Rig Veda* which state that before the universe 'there was neither non-existence nor existence'. Analogously, is it possible that there was neither darkness nor light? Is there another state beyond this dichotomy?

Action 3 Recount the ancient Greek story of Odysseus and Polyphemus. To escape the Cyclops's lair and avoid being eaten, Odysseus yanked out Polyphemus's one and only eyeball with a wooden stake.

    — *Question* 3 Can the eyeless Polyphemus see the dark?

       — If he can see the dark, what is he seeing it with?
       — If he can see the dark, is he truly blind?
       — If he were in a dark forest with us, would he see the same dark that we see?
       — Trees are likewise eyeless. Can they see the dark?
       — Are trees blind?
       — Are your knees blind?

    — *Question* 4 Have you ever seen the night?

       — Does everything you can see have a shape?
       — Does the night have a shape?
       — If you cannot see the night, how do you know it has arrived?
       — Is it the same night that returns at the end of every day?
       — Where do you have to look to see the night?
       — Can you see the night only when you are looking outside?
       — If so, then does the night only exist outside?

Solitaire

Topic Philosophers have speculated on the extent to which growing up in isolation might affect or limit us. The 18ᵗʰ century Scottish philosopher Adam Smith argued that without other people we would be incapable of morally evaluating our own actions and sentiments; other people provide a mirror through we can see and understand ourselves. In the 20ᵗʰ century, the philosopher Ludwig Wittgenstein added that such solitude would preclude speech because language requires a community of speakers.

This session continues the conversation by wondering whether, if marooned and alone, you'd still be able to tickle, and lie, and steal, and so on.

Props Mirror

Action 1 Ask the class to imagine that they were individually marooned on an uninhabited island. Though the predicament would surely preclude games of hide-and-seek, you're going to explore what other activities they might still be able to enjoy despite their isolation.

To start with, invite a volunteer to play 'it' by herself. (Enjoy the spectacle – it is highly entertaining!)

  — *Question* 1 Is it possible to run away from yourself? Is it possible to chase yourself?

    — Can you get any distance from yourself?
    — Can you leave yourself behind?

Action **2** Would you still have someone to fight? Ask a volunteer to push herself over.

    — *Question* **2** Is it possible to push yourself over?

        — If no, is this because you are not strong enough?

Action **3** Would you still have someone to climb over? Ask another volunteer to climb on top of herself.

    — *Question* **3** Is it possible to climb on top of yourself?

        — If no, is this because you are not agile enough?

Action **4** Would you still have someone to tickle? Ask another volunteer to tickle herself.

    — *Question* **4** Is it possible to tickle yourself?

        — Is it possible to overpower yourself?

Action **5** Would you still have someone to lie to? Ask another volunteer to look at herself in the mirror and say, 'You are a hippo'.

    — *Question* **5** Is it possible to lie to yourself?

Action **6** Would you still have someone to steal from? Ask another volunteer to try to steal her own shoes.

    — *Question* **6** Is it possible to steal from yourself?

Action **7** Would you still have someone to mimic? Ask a final volunteer to pretend to be herself.

— *Question* **7** Is it possible to pretend to be yourself?

> You can also explore this theme of isolation in relation to identity. If everyone disappeared and you were the only person alive, would certain aspects of your identity also disappear? For instance, if Usain Bolt was the only remaining person, would it still be true to describe him as fast, as Jamaican, as human? Can you have a talent of one? A nation of one? A species of one? Which aspects of our identity, if any, are intrinsic to us?

COALESCENCE

Topic According to Aristotle the ancient Greek philosopher Thales believed that all things were fundamentally composed of water. An alternative view from Democritus, another ancient Greek, claimed that everything is made of discrete indivisible entities called atoms.

Contrary to the atomic conception, one apparent implication of the Thalean view is that, like a confluence of rivers, all things can mix and merge. No individual is secure. Nothing can fortify itself against the essential fluidity of matter. This session explores these Thalean implications by asking whether people, and their shadows, can coalesce.

To illustrate what hermaphrodites are and so prime the class for the story of Action 3, consider showing them footage (which can be found online) from a David Attenborough documentary of two slugs mating. It's fascinating!

Props A torch

Action **1** Ask two volunteers (*x* and *y*) to place their hands before the whiteboard. Use a torch to make shadows of their hands. Ask them to bring their hands close enough together so that the two shadows begin to overlap.

— *Question* **1** How many shadows are there?

- — Can two people cast one shadow?
- — If there is one, consider: we speak of the shadows we cast as 'ours', we say that's 'my' shadow. So is the shadow of *y*'s pinkie now part of *x*'s shadow? Can *x* refer to this as her shadow?

Action **2** Ask two or three students to link arms and walk around the room in unison. Make a portmanteau out of their names.

— *Question* **2** Are they now one person?

> — If it is said they are two people because they have different thoughts, ask: If I have different thoughts at the same time, does that make me more than one person?
> — If it is said they are two people because they have different memories, ask: My memories today are different to yesterday (then I didn't remember yesterday, now I do). Does that mean that me-then and me-now are different people?
> — If it is said they are two people because they have two hearts, ask: If I acquired an additional heart, would that make me two people?

Action **3** Tell the story of Hermaphroditus (this can be found in Ovid's *Metamorphoses*). In brief, the nymph Salmacis, fired by desire, forcibly seized the beautiful young man Hermaphroditus (son of Hermes and Aphrodite) and implored the gods to ensure they would never be apart. The gods obliged by fusing their bodies into one. Here's one telling –

As the son of Aphrodite, Hermaphroditus was blessed with great beauty. No one could deny it. No one was immune to his radiance. Wherever he went he was the cynosure of attention. But on one strange and fateful day he crossed paths with the nymph Salmacis, and forever after, though he still turned heads, it was for an altogether different reason.

Much of that day had been unremarkable. He had hunted deer, as he often did, and the summer heat had been intense, as it often was. And after several hours of toil he had grown hot and weary and wanted to cool off, so he went in search of a lake. While on his way, he passed through a glade where he saw Salmacis in the centre singing to herself and dancing.

'Excuse me,' he said.

'Sorry, not today, very busy, thank you, bye bye' she

replied, without so much as looking at him.

'Please, I don't mean to bother you. I'm trying to find a lake.'

Annoyed at his persistence, Salmacis stopped with the firm intention of giving him what for. 'Now who do you think you – oh my...'

At the sight of his gorgeous face her anger disappeared.

'Do you know of a nearby lake?' he asked.

'Honey, baby, forget the lake – I've got other ideas for you.'

Hermaphroditus, realising that Salmacis would be of no use, turned to leave, but she, not known for her self-restraint, grabbed him by his tunic, pulled him towards her and growled, 'MARRY ME!'

He tried to recoil, but her grip only tightened. 'MARRY ME!' she repeated, and started to lick his face.

'Get off!' he cried, pulling away, 'I don't want to marry you! I don't want to marry anyone.'

Salmacis became suddenly contrite (she was prone to mood swings).

'Sorry! I don't know what came over me. Though, may I at least carry on licking you?'

'No! Leave me alone.'

'Fair enough,' she shrugged.

Hermaphroditus continued on his way, but the story doesn't end there.

Though Salmacis wanted to honour his request, she also found him utterly irresistible, and so, as a compromise, opted to follow him in secret while telling herself, 'Look but don't touch!'

This worked for a while. For close to an hour she

was content just to stare and wish. However, when Hermaphroditus reached the lake he made the grave mistake of removing his clothes.

Salmacis's jaw hit the ground. She wrapped her arms around a tree to try to control herself. As his naked body glided though the limpid water, she repeated over and over, 'Look but don't touch! Look but don't touch!' But this was more than she could be bear. Beating her head, grinding her teeth, rocking backwards and forwards – she realised that the only way to stop this madness was to give into it.

Moments later Hermaphroditus's peaceful swim was interrupted by a wild commotion near the shore. Looking over his shoulder he saw Salmacis speeding towards him. He swam away, aiming for the other side of the lake, but the distance between them rapidly closed, for where he had only fear to impel him, Salmacis was driven by a greater force, desire.

It wasn't long before she was able to reach out and grab his ankle. She pulled him towards her, reeling him in like a fish. He tried to get away but she wrapped her legs firmly around him.

'Get off me,' he cried.

'No! You're mine!'

In desperation, he started to gouge her eyes, pull her hair, anything to extricate himself. She struggled to maintain her grasp and soon only had hold of his hand. Feeling it slip away, she cried out to the gods, 'Gods, help! I beg of you – please ensure we will never be apart!'

The gods, who had been enjoying the spectacle from Mount Olympus, decided to grant her wish – and this is where things really started to get weird.

Despite being almost free of Salmacis, Hermaphroditus was unable to separate his hand from hers. It was as though they were glued together. He tried to force them apart but his skin just stretched and bounced back like rubber. Soon it became impossible to even stretch the skin. Their hands were merging. He noticed that the mole which had been on his thumb was now on hers, and the ring which had been on her finger was now on his – or was that still *his* thumb and *her* finger? He could no longer tell the difference. Indeed, after a few seconds there *was* no difference. Between them, they now only had three hands.

Next their arms fused together, and again their skin started to mix, and so did their muscles, and their veins began coiling round each other, and in one instant it felt as if his bone was being absorbed by hers, and in the next as if hers was being absorbed by his, till eventually they only had three arms between them.

The fusion didn't stop there. It continued across every inch of their bodies – merging tongues, blending eyeballs and two pounding hearts coalescing first in rhythm and then in substance – till only one body remained. To grant Salmacis's wish that she would never part from Hermaphroditus, the gods had united them in flesh and blood.

— *Question* **3** How many people is Hermaphroditus?

- — Can one body be two people?
- — Can one body have two minds?
- — Can one person have two minds?
- — Does Hermaphroditus still exist? Does Salmacis still exist?
- — If you were to kiss Hermaphorditus, how many people would you be kissing?

— *Question* **4** How many people are you?

- — How can you tell how many people you are?
- — How many minds do you have? How do you know?
- — Could you be wrong about how many people you are?

LOOKING

Topic The philosopher of art Kendall Walton believes that photographs have a property he calls 'transparency'. He believes that when you look at a photograph of an object you are literally looking at that object. The photograph is 'transparent' because you see right through it to the object itself. If we talk of seeing objects through binoculars and glasses, why not say that we can see them through photographs?

Dominic McIver Lopes goes one step further and argues that when we look at a drawing or a painting of someone, we are literally seeing that person. When you look at, say, Leonardo's Mona Lisa, you are not seeing a depiction of Lisa del Giocondo but Lisa del Giocondo herself!

This lesson addresses these ideas through the story of Perseus and Medusa.

Props A drawing of Medusa and a mirror

Action **1** Tell the story of Perseus of Medusa. In brief, Perseus was told that the only way he could save his mother from being forced to marry King Polydectes – a man whom she didn't love – was by decapitating Medusa and brining Polydectes the head.

For the sake of his mother he embarked on this perilous mission knowing full well the legend of the serpent-haired Medusa: whoever looked her in the eye was petrified by her ugliness and turned instantly to stone.

 Present a drawing of Medusa.

— *Question* 1 If Perseus looked at a drawing of Medusa, would he turn to stone?

  — When he looks at a drawing of Medusa, is he looking at her?
  — Is she present in her portraits?

Action 2 Pretend that you have a photograph of Medusa in your pocket which you are reluctant to show the class lest they calcify.

— *Question* 2 If Perseus looked at a photograph of Medusa, would he turn to stone?

  — When he looks at a photograph of Medusa, is he looking at her?
  — 'He can't possibly be looking at her because in the photograph she is only 5cm tall but in real life she is over 5ft tall.' Is this a good argument?
  — Is she present in her selfies?

Action 3 Hold up a mirror to the class.

— *Question* 3 If Perseus looked at the reflection of Medusa, would he turn to stone?

  — When he looks at the reflection of Medusa, is he looking at her?
  — Is she present in her reflection?

You can explore the audio analogue of the mirror question by discussing echoes: if you hear the echo of a person's voice, have you heard the person's voice? If you hear both the voice and the echo, have you heard two sounds or one? Do the answers offered here equate to the answer given in the case of looking at a visual reflection? If not, what's the difference? To further explore the similarities or differences, you can ask whether listening to a recording of a person's voice constitutes listening to the person's voice. Again, if the answer here does not equate to the answer given in the corresponding question regarding the photograph, why not? What's the difference?

Action 4 Finally, using the mirror to experiment with, you can explore the implications of answering 'no' to the previous questions by asking –

    – *Question* 4 Have you ever seen your face?

        – Is it possible for Medusa to turn herself to stone?
        – Is it possible for an eye to see itself?

CONTRADICTION

Topic Following Aristotle's lead, many philosophers have embraced the so-called Law of Contradiction, a principle which states that contradictions can never be true. According to Aristotle there are no situations under which a contradictory statement, such as 'We all live in a yellow submarine but some of us don't', can be true. Though this may seem like common sense, some philosophers do advocate dialetheism, which is the view that contradictions can be true (not all contradictions, it should be said, only some – they are not committed to saying that dialetheism is also false).

This session enters the mix by considering whether we can be in two places at once. If this is possible, then contradictions can seemingly be true. If, for instance, you stood straddling the border between England and Scotland, arguably you'd be both in Scotland and not in Scotland.

Props None

Action **1** Ask a volunteer (*x*) to stand with one foot inside the classroom and the other outside it.

– *Question* **1** Is *x* in two places at the same time?

- If she is in neither, where is she?
- If a part of her is inside and a part of her is outside, where is she?
- If she is inside and not inside, does that mean she is where she isn't?

You can also do this with so-called scattered objects, such as you lunch. Place one part of your lunch – banana, say – outside of the classroom, and the other part – sandwich, say – inside the classroom and ask, 'Is my lunch in two places at the same time?'

Action **2** Now ask the class to pretend that *x* is standing at the border between France and Spain with one foot inside each country, and while standing there she commits a crime.

— *Question* **2** Should the French or Spanish police arrest her?

— Where did *x* commit the crime?
— Do the borders between countries have width?
— Is it possible to have a line without width?

IMAGINATION

Topic Some philosophers regard conceivability as a guide to possibility: what we can imagine is an indication of what can be, while what we cannot imagine is an indication of what cannot be. The medieval philosopher Thomas Aquinas, for instance, argued that since contradictory objects, such as round squares, are impossible to imagine, not even an omnipotent being such as God could create them.

René Descartes, on the other hand, claimed that the limits of imagination do not correspond to the limits of possibility. An omnipotent being may well have the power to create round squares. According to Descartes, there is more to reality than our minds can fathom; or, as the biologist J.B.S. Haldane famously said, 'It is my suspicion that the universe is not only queerer than we suppose, but queerer than we can suppose'.

Props None

Action Tell the class that they are going to test the limits of their imaginations. They are going to explore whether there is anything it is impossible to imagine. With each of these tasks, ask them to close their eyes for 10 seconds.

> — *Question* 1 Can you imagine being the sky?
>
>> — If yes, what is it like?
>> — How is it different to being a human?

— *Question* **2** Can you imagine not being anywhere?

- — If yes, what is it like?
- — If no, why is it unimaginable?
- — Is it impossible?

— *Question* **3** Can you imagine not having a body?

- — If yes, how is it different to having a body?
- — If no, why is it unimaginable?
- — Is it impossible?

— *Question* **4** Can you imagine having three bodies?

- — If yes, how is it different to having one body?
- — If no, why is it unimaginable?
- — Is it impossible?
- — Can you imagine having three different conversations at the same time with three different mouths?

— *Question* **5** Can you imagine giving birth to yourself?

- — If yes, can you draw it?
- — If no, why is it unimaginable?
- — Is it impossible?

— *Question* **6** Can you imagine nothingness?

- — If yes, can you describe it?
- — If no, why is it unimaginable?
- — Does it exist?
- — Is imagining nothing the same as not imagining anything?

MOTION

Topic Among the ancient Greek philosophers the reality of motion was a divisive issue. Whereas Parmenides and Zeno of Elea argued that, contrary to appearance, there is no motion in the world, Epicurus claimed, again, contrary to appearance, that everything is fundamentally always in motion. In modern times, Friedrich Engels, Karl Marx's collaborator, siding with the Epicureans wrote, 'Matter without motion is just as unthinkable as motion without matter'.

Props Ball (though any object will do)

Action **1** Ask a volunteer to hold the ball and walk around the classroom.

— *Question* **1** Is the ball moving?

Action **2** Inform the class that in its orbit of the sun, the earth is travelling through space at a speed of 67,000 miles an hour.

— *Question* **2** Is your nose moving at 67,000 miles an hour?

- — Is your nose orbiting the sun?
- — If yes, does that mean your nose is travelling faster than an aeroplane?

Action **3** Present the following two statements:

The wind *has* motion.
The wind *is* motion.

— *Question* **3** Which statement is correct?

— Can the wind be still? Can it exist without motion?

Action 4 Ask a volunteer (*x*) to walk from one side of the room to the other. Midway through ask her to freeze and stand as still as a statue. Ask the class to imagine that she never moved again and remained this way forever, without a heartbeat or blood flow, without change or growth.

    — *Question* 4 Does *x* still exist?

        — Can we live without motion?
        — Are you looking at a person when you look at the statue?
        — Is the statue a corpse?

Action 5 Inform the class that according to according to physics, the particles that make up solids are always in motion (they vibrate). Present an object to the class, the ball for instance, and ask –

    — *Question* 5 If every particle in the ball is in motion, is the ball in motion?

        — Is anything in the world entirely still?
        — Can you hold a thought entirely still?

You could explore this final question by examining the fallacy of composition. According to this principle it is erroneous to infer that the whole has a given property because its parts have that same property. For example, it is erroneous to infer that the beach is small because every pebble on the beach is small. But is this inference from the parts to the whole always wrong? It seems correct, for example, to say that if every item of clothing in the wash pile stinks, then the wash pile stinks. Are there other examples? And is the case described in the Question 5 such an example?

FRANGIBILITY

Topic Because of its contemplative nature philosophy is sometimes referred to as an armchair discipline, but this needn't imply that it's somehow inactive – there's a lot that you can do in an armchair. It needn't be all chin-stroking and reverie; it can be messy and frenetic, as this lesson may well attest.

This lesson involves what one might call 'experimental metaphysics'. It takes a concept, frangibility, and tests its limits, exploring how far it can be stretched and to what it can be applied.

Props A bottle of water

Action **1** Invite a volunteer to attempt to break the water inside the bottle.

— *Question* **1** Can water be broken?

- — Does water have parts?
- — If we divide the water into two containers, has it been broken?
- — Can you chew water?
- — Though we might say 'This is a stone', why does it not sound right to say 'This is a water'?
- — If smashed stone fragments could merge back together as seamlessly as water, would we think that stones couldn't be broken?
- — Does water have a function we can sabotage?
- — If we boil it away, are we breaking it?
- — If we freeze it and break the ice, have we broken it?

Action **2** Pour the water out of the bottle and invite another volunteer to attempt to break the air inside the empty bottle.

— *Question* **2** Can air be broken?

  — Is air already broken?
  — Does air have parts?
  — Can you chew air?
  — Though we might say 'This is a stone', why does it not sound right to say 'This is an air'?
  — Does air have a function we can sabotage?

Action **3** Given the combustibility of children, I'd advise against using a volunteer for this question. For illustrative purposes, however, you could simply strike a match.

— *Question* **3** Can fire be broken?

  — Does fire have parts?
  — Is extinguishing fire the same as breaking it?
  — Can you smash fire?
  — Does fire have a function we can sabotage?

> To enrich your students' lexicons and help revive an endangered word, one that has been in mortal decline since the late 18th century, you could introduce 'adamantine' into the discussion. When John Milton described the 'adamantine chains' of Satan's internment, he was referring to supernatural substances within a supernatural realm. But is there any terrestrial substance of comparable brawniness? Are there any adamantine things within the natural world?

ANNIHILATION

Topic Following **FRANGIBILITY**, here's another session to delight (or frustrate) students of destructive appetites. Here the aim isn't merely to break but to annihilate!

The first action, focusing on the destruction of a poem, may be harder than it first appears. The English philosopher and archaeologist R. G. Collingwood claimed that poems, indeed all art works, are not physical but imaginary things. The words on the page are not the poem itself but the poem's medium, the means by which we can access the poet's imaginary composition. So to annihilate a poem would require the annihilation of an imaginary thing.

Props A printed copy of any poem and a cardboard box of any size

Action 1 Read the poem to the class before asking a volunteer to try to destroy it. Following the attempt, ask –

– *Question* 1 Has the poem been destroyed?

- – Does the poem still exist?
- – If you destroyed every copy of the poem, would it still exist?
- – Is the poem on the page or is it somewhere else?
- – Can everything that was once created also be destroyed?

Action 2 Place a cardboard box before the class and ask a volunteer to try to destroy the space inside it.

— *Question* **2** Has the space inside the box been destroyed?

- Does the space still exist?
- Is destroying the box the same as destroying the space within it?
- Is filling the space a form of destruction?
- As the box is moved from one side of the classroom to the other, is the space within it the same space?
- Can space be created?

Action **3** Ask everyone in the class to cup their hands together to create a sort of dark hollow, leaving an opening at the top so they can look into it. Ask them to behold the darkness, then after a moment, ask them to separate their hands.

— *Question* **3** Has the darkness been destroyed?

- If darkness is an absence, is it possible to destroy an absence?
- If darkness is a nothing, is it possible to destroy a nothing?
- If the universe were destroyed, would darkness remain?
- If you re-cup your hands, has the same darkness returned?

You could further explore the second subsidiary question by considering the origin of the universe. If prior to the universe there was nothingness, did its creation thereby involve the annihilation of nothingness? More generally, by creating something are you annihilating its prior absence? By creating his statue David was Michelangelo annihilating the absence of David? By lighting a candle, are you annihilating the absence of the flame? Does this notion of annihilating absence make sense? Or, to explore the question from a different angle, does every act of creation necessarily involve destruction? Does the painter destroy the blank canvas? Did Michelangelo destroy the formless marble?

Action 4 Place a clock or watch before the class and ask them to imagine how they could go about destroying time.

— *Question* 4 Can you destroy a minute?

— As time passes is it continuously destroying itself?
— Can you destroy a minute in less than a minute?

— *Question* 5 Can the school be destroyed?

— Is destroying the building the same as destroying the school?
— Is the school the building?
— Is the school the people?
— Is the school the name?

A more fitting word to use in this session would be 'annihilate'. If you think some of your students may not be familiar or comfortable with that word, then 'destroy' is still fine. However, it could be an opportune moment to introduce the word, and if they are already familiar with it, to start the session by briefly looking at its etymology: from ad nihil, Latin for 'to nothing', so effectively, 'to reduce to nothing'.

PURPOSE

Topic Aristotle wrote that when an eye loses its sight it is no longer an eye. This comment invites two conflicting views. On the one hand, that objects are defined by their uses. And on the other, that they are defined by their purposes. According to the first view an object is defined by what it can do, and to the second by what it is for. That is to say, its nature is either changing and contingent or fixed and ingrained.

Props A fork, for illustrative purposes

Action 1 Tell a story of three Chinese explorers who travelled to Italy in the 15th century and encountered a new and unfamiliar object: something the Italians call una forchetta. The three explorers puzzled over what it might be. The first speculated that it was a back scratcher, the second a hairbrush (or 'dinglehopper' to aficionados of *The Little Mermaid*), while the third believed it was a tool for eating with.

   — *Question* 1 Which explorer was right?

- When it is being used as a hairbrush, does it become a hairbrush?
- Is it many things or just one thing?
- Is it always a fork (a thing for eating with) no matter how it is used?
- If it becomes the thing it is being used as, what is it when it's not being used?
- If one of the explorers is using one of the objects as a hairbrush while another explorer is using another one to scratch his back with, are they holding different objects?

> Feel free to use different objects in the story. Anything will do. You could even present an uncommon kitchen utensil and ask the class to guess what it might be. The philosophical point you're addressing is whether a thing's nature and identity is determined by how it is used or by something else entirely; the intentions of its maker, for instance. There are implications for both views and the questions below address each. Question 2 is tailored for those who answer that all three explorers were right and that use does determine nature, while Question 3 is for those who believe that the intentions of a thing's maker, the purpose it is made to fulfil, determines its intrinsic nature.

Action 2 Ask for two volunteers to role-play. One child (*x*) is in the park on all-fours looking for worms (a budding entomologist). The other child is a blind person out for a walk. The blind person becomes tired and wishes to rest. Mistaking the entomologist for a bench, he sits on her.

— *Question* 2 Is *x* a bench?

- When being used as a bench, does *x* become a bench?
- When being used as a bench, is *x* still a human?
- Is *x* both a human and a bench?
- Can only *x* tell us what she is?
- If *x* consented to being used as a bench, would she then be a bench?

Action 3 Tell the story of a lazy couple who hated washing up. So contemptuous were they of the chore, they decided to have a child just so they could raise it to wash the dishes. Since their surname was Washer, they naturally named the child Dish, and from her earliest years Dish was trained to wash up. That's all she ever did. She stood at the sink scrubbing and wiping. After all, that's what she was made for.

— *Question* 3 Is Dish Washer a dish washer?

- Is Dish Washer the creation of her parents?

— Who is Dish Washer's creator?
— Does Dish Washer have a purpose?
— Do your parents determine your purpose?

ART

Topic Among philosophers there are many disagreements about what art is and where its value resides. R. G. Collingwood believed that art involves the expression of emotion whereas Clive Bell claimed that art is not constituted by the emotions it expresses but rather the emotions it evokes. Ignoring emotion altogether, George Dickie argues that art is simply whatever an art gallery chooses to exhibit, be it a Bernini sculpture or a mound of bellybutton fluff. This lesson enters the fray by trying to understand what art is *not*.

Props A pencil and two sheets of paper for each student

Action **1** Give the class one minute to make a piece of art using the pencil and one sheet of paper. Ask different volunteers to take turns presenting their work and ask –

   – *Question* **1** Is this art?

> With this question you are trying to arrive at a definition of art, to identify its ingredients. When responding to a child's contribution, generalise from her thought regarding this specific example to all art e.g. if she says, 'It is art because it's pretty,' ask, 'Are you saying that for something to be art it has to be pretty?' You're trying to guide the child from a particular observation to a general principle, helping her to realise that she's not only noticed something about this specific drawing, she's potentially realised something about the nature of art itself.

Action **2** Give the class one minute to make a piece of 'non-art' – something that most certainly isn't art – using the pencil and the second sheet of paper. Ask different volunteers to take turns presenting their work and ask –

— *Question* **2** Is this non-art?

- If everything is art, does everything have an artist?
- If everything is art, does the word 'art' mean anything?
- Is there anything that doesn't belong in a gallery?
- Is 'Make non-art' an impossible instruction?

> This lesson structure is applied to music in the bean below. It could, moreover, be used to explore the nature of dance. This would be a matter of asking your students to create short non-dance shows.

MUSIC

Topic This session repeats the structure of **ART** but applies it to music.

Props Miscellaneous classroom items such as scissors and pencils

Action **1** Distribute a couple of miscellaneous classroom objects to each student. Inform them that these are their instruments and that they have 30 seconds to try to compose a piece of music. Ask a volunteer to present her composition –

— *Question* **1** Is this music?

Action **2** Give the class one minute to make a piece of 'non-music' – something that most certainly isn't music – using the same objects. Ask a volunteer to present her work –

— *Question* **2** Is this non-music?

- — Can music be silent?
- — Can music be random?
- — Is there a difference between sound and music?

Music in the 20th century came with an abundance of curious moments. There was John Cage's famous 4' 33", a three movement piece in which the performer does nothing, Steve Reich's *It's Gonna Rain*, which consists of a looped and phased clip of a preacher's voice, La Monte Young's *Poem for Chairs, Tables, Benches, Etc., or Other Sound Sources*, in which performers drag various pieces of furniture across the floor, George Brecht's *Drip Music*, in which water drips into an empty container, and Robert Watts's *Duet for Tuba*, in which coffee and cream are dispensed from a tuba's spit valves, to name a few.

Given that performances of many such pieces can be found online, after the final question – I wouldn't suggest looking at these before since it may pre-empt or foreclose the students' own thoughts and experimentalism – you could play a few (in addition to John Cage's 4' 33", I'd recommend his 1960 *Water Walk*) and ask the class whether it thinks they are music.

You could also expand the session by considering whether music is an exclusively human phenomenon. For instance, you could play clips of falling rain, buzzing bees or singing birds, and in each case ask whether it constitutes music.

NATURE

Topic The belief that there is a distinction between the natural and unnatural has been used throughout history to justify and impose behavioural norms. Thomas Aquinas, for instance, based his entire understanding of what is right and wrong on this distinction, arguing that cannibalism, to cite one example, is wrong because it's unnatural. The legitimacy of this distinction can, therefore, have significant consequences for how we view and act in the world.

Props A bar of chocolate, a wooden spoon, a phone and a banana – feel free to experiment with different objects

Action 1 Place the objects on the floor in a horizontal line. Taking volunteers –

> — *Question* 1 Can you arrange these objects in a line from the most natural to the least?
>
>> — If being man-made renders something unnatural, is that also true for animal-made things such as spiderwebs and beaver dams?
>> — Is there anything less natural than these objects?
>> — Is there anything more natural than these objects?

With the first subsidiary question, you can easily experiment with new items by drawing them on sheets of paper and introducing them. With the second and third questions, you can distribute sheets of paper or small whiteboards and ask students to illustrate the objects they're thinking of and then invite them to add these to the spectrum for others to see.

You can also specify that they can use the spacing between the objects to illustrate the different degrees of naturalness.

Action **2** Ask for new volunteers to show where they think *they* belong on the spectrum –

— *Question* **2** Are you more or less natural than these objects?

— Are you man-made?
— What could you change to make yourself either more or less natural?

Action **3** To move from objects to actions: ask four students to stand in a horizontal line, each one assuming a different pose to illustrate a particular action: getting dressed, eating, murdering and performing surgery. Feel free to make these actions more specific (for instance, eating a human leg or an apple; killing an attacking bear or an innocent person; putting knickers on your head or a scarf around your neck) or experiment with different actions altogether. Taking volunteers –

— *Question* **3** Can you arrange these actions in a line from the most natural to the least?

— If we are natural, does that mean that everything we do is natural?

WRONGNESS

Topic Ethics is the branch of philosophy concerned with questions of how we should live and what we should value. To give one example, the late 18th century philosopher Jeremy Bentham – whose desiccated body remains preserved and on display at University College London – believed that pleasure was the only valuable thing in the world. He believed that we should devote our lives to producing as much pleasure as we can for as many people as possible.

This lesson invites the class to generate their own random moral questions, which they can then use to discover their own ethical principles.

Props Word cards

Action **1** One set of word cards contains a list of verbs and the other a list of nouns. You can experiment with different of possibilities. The lists below are merely suggestions –

Verbs	Nouns
Spit on	An elephant
Marry	A tree
Murder	A spider
Lie to	A baby
Steal from	Yourself
Swear at	The Queen

Separate the verb and noun word cards into separate piles. Place a card on the floor that reads 'Is it wrong to…' Ask one child to choose a random word from the verb pile and place it on the floor. Ask another child to choose a random word from the noun pile and place it beside the verb. Repeat this till both piles are empty and you have a set of six questions.

— *Question* **1** Are any of these actions wrong?

— Are any of these actions impossible? (e.g. Is it possible to steal from yourself?)

> You can explore a given answer by using the word cards to consider alternative actions. For instance, if one of the questions that emerges is 'Is it wrong to spit on the Queen?', and a student highlights this as the most egregious act, you can follow this up by asking whether it would still be wrong if we replaced 'The Queen' with 'A baby'. Whichever way the student answers, asking them 'Why?' will help to illuminate their thinking e.g. spitting on the Queen is wrong because she is important and we shouldn't disrespect important people, or it's wrong because she is a person and we shouldn't disrespect anybody. Of course, this latter reason presents further possible follow-ups, for instance, would it still be wrong if 'A baby' was replaced with 'An elephant', and so on.

Action **2** To move from randomness to design: ask volunteers to rearrange the word cards to produce the action that they believe is the most wrong.

— *Question* **2** Is this action the most wrong?

Action **3** Invite volunteers to try to rearrange the cards to make *all* of the actions wrong.

— *Question* **3** Are all of these actions wrong?

Action **4** Invite volunteers to try to rearrange the cards to make *none* of the actions wrong.

— *Question* **4** Are none of these actions wrong?

POSSIBILITY

Topic This session uses the set-up of **WRONGNESS** to generate random metaphysical questions. Whereas ethics is concerned with value and action, metaphysics is concerned with existence and reality. In other words, metaphysics tries to understand what the world is rather than how we should live in it.

Many of these questions are touched upon in other sessions, but this format offers a more spontaneous way to explore them.

Props Word cards

Action **1** One set of word cards contains a list of verbs and the other a list of nouns. You can experiment with different possibilities. The lists below are merely suggestions –

Verbs	Nouns
Break	Colour
Create	Sound
Destroy	Light
Touch	Darkness
Shrink	Thoughts
Enlarge	Silence

Separate the verb and noun word cards into separate piles. Place a card on the floor that reads 'Is it possible to...' Ask one child to choose a random word from the verb pile and place it on the floor. Ask another child to choose a random word from the noun pile and place it beside the verb. Repeat this till both piles are empty and you have set of six questions.

— *Question* 1 Are any of these actions possible?

    — What would have to change for it to become possible?

Action 2 Ask volunteers to rearrange the word cards to produce the action that they believe is impossible.

    — *Question* 2 Is this action impossible?

Action 3 Invite volunteers to try to rearrange the cards to make *all* of the actions possible.

    — *Question* 3 Are all of these actions possible?

Action 4 Invite volunteers to try to rearrange the cards to make *none* of the actions possible.

    — *Question* 4 Are none of these actions possible?

PROPERTY

Topic The English philosopher John Locke argued that if you found an apple tree on an uninhabited island and plucked off one of its apples, you would thereby own that apple. By virtue of plucking the fruit it has become 'mixed' with your body and your labour and is consequently yours.

This lesson explores the implications of taking an item that someone has already laid claim to and then mixing it with your body in ways more intimate than plucking. It challenges the foundation and crucial presupposition of Locke's argument, namely, that our body is our property.

Props Unopened bottle of water

Action **1** Invite a volunteer (*x*) to help you perform this little drama: having bought a bottle of water on a sultry day you place it in your jacket pocket and walk through the park. While walking you become absorbed in a difficult philosophical problem and so lose awareness of your surroundings. *x* notices this and seizes the opportunity – she swipes the bottle and flees. (To tease and entertain, make it difficult for *x* by suddenly walking in different directions.)

— *Question* **1** Does *x* now own the water?

— If something is in your possession, do you own it?

Action **2** Ask *x* to open the bottle and take a gulp.

— *Question* **2** Does *x* now own *this* *pointing to her belly* water?

- If *x* had broken into a jeweller's and swallowed the diamond rings, would she own them?
- Do we own everything inside us?
- If I still own it, could I sell it?
- If I still own it, would it be OK for me to forcibly try to get it back?

> If you fancy getting mythological, you can tie in the story of Cronus who was told by an oracle that he would be murdered by one of his children and so swallowed five of his newborn babies (he eventually threw them back up). Of course, some may be inclined to say that Cronus already owned the babies since they were 'his', but the myth could be modified such that while in the maternity ward he haplessly gobbled the wrong tot.

Action 3 Point out that for those who say she owns the water once it is in her belly, they are presupposing that she is in fact the owner of 'her' belly.

- *Question* 3 Does *x* own *this* *pointing* belly?

  - Did she buy it?
  - Did she make it?
  - Is she responsible for it?
  - Is she in control of it?
  - Do her parents own it?
  - If her mum owns it, does that mean her mum has two bellies?
  - Does God own it?
  - If God owns it, does that mean that when *x* eats too much jam, God has a sore belly?
  - If we don't own our belly, or our hands for that matter, and if someone were to surgically remove 'our' hands during the night, would that be an act of theft?

POSSESSION

Topic The French philosopher Simone Weil believed that there is a crucial fact about our existence we cannot bear to acknowledge, namely, that 'I may lose at any moment, through the play of circumstances over which I have no control, anything whatsoever that I possess, including those things which are so intimately mine that I consider them as being myself.'

Though Weil stressed that we can lose anything we possess, Immanuel Kant argued that not all of it is up for sale: there are certain things that we should never trade away. Specifically, he argued that we should not sell our body parts because our body is not our property. To regard our body as property is to think of it as an object, but people are not objects, nor should they be treated as such.

Props A wad of rectangular pieces of plain paper

Action Tell the class that this is magical paper: whatever sum of money you write on it, the paper becomes that amount. Ask *x* how much she'd like for her shoelaces, and *y* for his house, and *z* for his elbows, and so on. Distribute the riches as you go.

— *Question* **1** Is there anything you have which is impossible to sell?

- — Can you sell your voice?
- — Can you sell your name?
- — Can you sell your memories?
- — Is there anything that could never be stolen from you?

— *Question* **2** Is there anything you have which it would be wrong to sell?

- — Is it wrong to sell a gift?
- — Is it wrong to sell a pet?
- — Is it wrong to sell yourself?

HARMLESS ACTS

Topic In ethics, consequentialism is the view that the moral value of an act is determined by its consequences: if an act has no negative consequences, then it's morally permissible. This is in contrast to a deontological approach which holds that the consequences are irrelevant: actions in themselves are either good or bad.

This session explores these different outlooks while mixing in considerations about ownership.

Action 1 Tell the story of a young man who keeps a ring that was worn by his dead grandmother in a small wooden box. Finding the sight of it too painful, the memories too vivid, only on occasion does he shake the box to reassure himself of its presence. He never opens the lid.

A friend of the man, who knows of the ring and is aware of its enormous value, decides one day to steal and sell it. Not wanting to distress or upset his friend, the thief decides to replace the ring with a coin, and the plan works perfectly. Whenever the man shakes the box, it feels and sounds exactly the same. The theft is never discovered.

— *Question* 1 Did the friend do anything wrong?

- — Has the friend done any harm?
- — Did the friend act considerately?

There are many other similar stories and scenarios you can present which describe actions that seemingly have no painful consequences. For example, is it wrong to stand at the foot of your parents' bed while they sleep and swear at them? Or to read a friend's messages without their knowledge? Or, if you found a totally unique and astonishingly beautiful flower buried in the depths of the jungle in a location no other person would ever find, would it be wrong to trample all over this one-of-a-kind wonder? If so, why? Is a loss still a loss when no one is aware of it?

Action 2 Outline the details of the discovery of Tutankhamun's tomb in 1922 by the archaeologist Howard Carter. Within the tomb were thousands of the pharaoh's possessions, including exquisitely crafted pieces of jewellery which the Egyptians believed he would take with him to the afterlife. These treasures, however, were taken from the tomb, some even from his body, and have since been displayed in museums around the world.

— *Question* 2 Was it wrong to take these objects from Tutankhamun's tomb?

- Is it theft?
- Is Tutankhamun their owner?
- Does the public have a right to see them?
- Does Tutankhamun have any rights?
- Is it possible to harm the dead?

Action 3 Present this argument to the class –

The dead cannot own anything, so to take from them is not stealing.

— *Question* 3 Is this correct?

Action 4 Present the details of the case of Simon Bramhall, the surgeon who marked his initials onto the livers of his unconscious patients without their consent.

Imagine that the initials were never discovered and that his patients went about their lives without any knowledge of what he had done to them. In this alternative world –

– *Question* **4** Did the surgeon do anything wrong?

- If no, would it also not be wrong to tattoo a blind person without their knowledge?
- If a patient did discover the initials, but actually quite liked having them, would that mean his actions weren't wrong?

INSIDES

Topic The 20th century American philosopher David Lewis believed that every possible world exists. There is, for instance, a world in which your doppelgänger has webbed hands and eats food through its anus. Since such a world is possible, according to Lewis it must exist.

An altogether less peculiar idea – notwithstanding Arthur Rimaud's thought 'Je est un autre' – of Lewis's was that 'Everything is identical to itself; nothing is ever identical to anything except itself'. This lesson, however, goes beyond the claim that everything is self-identical and considers the idea that everything is self-contained.

Props A glass jar and a sock

Action **1** Present a glass jar for all to see and ask –

— *Question* **1** Is there glass inside the jar?

— If the glass is inside the jar, what is it contained by?

Action **2** Tell the class to look around the room and ask –

— *Question* **2** Are there walls inside this room?

— 'The walls *are* the room'/ 'The walls are *part* of the room' – which statement is correct?

Action 3 Show the class the inside of a sock and present the following argument –

When you look inside the sock you are still looking at a sock, therefore the sock is inside itself.

— *Question* 3 Is this true?

Action 4 Present the following clues and ask the class to solve the riddle –

You are the only person in the world who will ever see me.
When you see me, you do not recognise me. You only know it was me after I have gone.
If you explored the world, you would never find me.
When you are inside me I am inside you.

What am I?

The answer is 'Your dreams'. Ask the class whether they disagree with any of the clues i.e. do any mischaracterise dreams? After taking a few thoughts, focus on the last point by presenting this statement to the class –

When you sleep you enter into dreams, and those dreams are inside you, so when you dream you are inside yourself.

— *Question* 4 Is this true?

You can also explore these questions of containment by looking at the story of how young Krishna's mother looked inside his mouth and saw the entire universe, including herself: 'She saw within the body of her son, in his gaping mouth, the whole universe in all its variety, with all the forms of life and time and nature and action and hopes, and her own village, and herself.' One question this raises is whether it actually makes sense. Is it possible for the universe to be wholly inside something which itself is wholly inside the universe? Can this be imagined?

— *Question* **5** Are you always inside something?

- — Are you always inside yourself?
- — Is there anything it's impossible to leave?
- — Are you inside the universe?
- — If the universe has no outside, does it have an inside?

Since Question 5 has no corresponding Action to contextualise it, I'd recommend writing it up on the board. The question itself is acting as its own stimulus and so it needs to be present in the room, something the students can see. And generally, in such cases, size matters. The larger and more imposing the lettering, the more intriguing and immediate the question will seem.

WONDERFUL WORLD

Topic The German philosopher and mathematician G. W. Leibniz argued that we live in the best of all possible worlds. Given God's perfection, He would not have created anything less than the best. Though we may sometimes despair at the suffering in this world, according to Leibniz there could be none better. This lesson explores this contention by presenting a twist on the ancient Greek myth of Pandora.

Props A jar/ box, slips of paper

Action Using about eight slips of paper, write down a range of seemingly negative features of life, for example, illness, accidents, aging, death, jealousy, hatred, sadness and pain. Fold these up and place them in the jar.

Tell the story of Pandora's jar, specifically, of how Zeus filled the jar with malign spirits designed to vitiate human life. Once you've told the class of how Pandora opened the jar and released the spirits, invite volunteers to remove the slips of paper to discover what they were.

With the slips of paper on the floor, tell the class that you are going to give the myth a twist. Ask them to imagine that Zeus was (rather uncharacteristically) overcome with guilt for what he had done, and so he gave Pandora the option of returning one spirit to the jar. Once returned, that scourge would disappear forever.

— *Question* What would you put back in the jar?

   — Referring to their choice: Is *x* ever good?
     (e.g. Is pain ever good?)
   — Would removing that spirit cause any of the others to
     disappear?

Once your class is familiar with the format of this lesson, you can run it again, forgoing the storytelling and experimenting with different banes, bales and tribulations e.g. foul smells, horrid tastes, punishments, coldness, anger, boredom, ugliness, waiting, hunger, darkness, fear, breakages, confusion, loneliness, fear, embarrassment, shame, and so on.

CLOTHES

Topic This session considers where our bodies end and our clothes begin, and where our clothes end and the world begins. To take one view, it is written in the ancient Hindu text the *Bhagavad Gita* that our bodies are like clothes, temporary garments worn by the eternal self: 'Just as one throws out old clothes and then takes on other new ones, so the embodied self casts out old bodies as it gets other new ones.'

Props None

Action 1 Describe to the class the biblical description of Adam and Eve in the Garden of Eden: naked and frolicking among vegetarian lions and beasts, blessed with a bounty of fruit. Focusing on the detail of their nudity, address each of the following items (*x*):

Hats   Socks
Glasses   Sunblock
Rings   Perfume
A rucksack   A fig leaf

— *Question* 1 Might the naked Adam and Eve have been wearing *x*?

- — Is someone who is wearing only *x* naked?
- — How many items can be combined while still preserving their nudity?
- — Did Adam and Eve have hair? Does hair impair nudity?
- — If Adam went bald, would that make him more naked?
- — If Eve has more freckles than Adam, does that mean she is less naked than he is?
- — Is nudity a matter of degrees?

Action 2 Ask the class to mention or write down everything they are wearing. Whatever items they mention, move from the whole to the parts e.g.

— *Question* 2 Are you wearing pockets?

- Are you wearing shoelaces?
- Are you wearing zips?
- Are you wearing buttons?

Action 3 I'll leave it for you to decide whether you ask for volunteers to illustrate the next question...

— *Question* 3 When you give someone a piggyback, are you wearing them?

- While you drive a car, are you wearing it?
- While you are in bed, are you wearing it?

Action 4 Show the class an image of a lion.

— *Question* 4 Is the lion naked?

- Is its fur a form of clothing?
- Is its fur part of its body?
- Is it clothed by its own body?
- Is the moon naked?

— *Question* 5 Are you wearing a face?

- Are you wearing skin?
- Are you wearing eyebrows?
- Are your eyebrows *on* your body or *part* of your body?
- Are you wearing hands?

HOME

Topic In the Book of Leviticus God says that we are 'strangers and foreigners' on earth. St Paul in his letters writes that we are 'citizens of heaven'. And the early Christian theologian Cyprian of Carthage described Christians as merely sojourning in this world.

The characterisation of humans as cosmically homeless is a recurring theme in religious texts. Contrariwise, the ancient Greek philosopher Diogenes, who had no permanent residence, proudly declared that he was a 'cosmopolitan', a citizen of the world.

These questions of home are questions of our connection to the land and the earth. Are we earthlings or here in exile? What land is our land? Where are the boundaries of our belonging?

Props An umbrella (for illustrative purposes)

Action **1** With an umbrella in hand and open, ask the class what it is and what it can be used for. After several contributions, ask –

— *Question* **1** Could it be a person's home?

- — Do homes require an inside? A kind of containment?
- — Do homes require privacy?
- — Do homes require permanence?
- — Is there a difference between being under and inside an umbrella?

Action **2** Present the following argument to the class –

1. The universe is my home.

2. The parts of one's home are also one's home.

3. Buckingham Palace is part of the universe.

4. Therefore, Buckingham Palace is my home.

— *Question 2* Is this correct?

- If the universe is not our home, and it is all there is, does that mean we are homeless?
- Do homes require a border?
- Is the universe where you belong?
- Is reality your home?

Action 3 Ask the class to imagine a woman who read the above argument and became so convinced of its truth that she packed her things and broke into Buckingham Palace. She found a large room with an agreeable colour scheme, made herself comfortable and there she lived for many years.

So capacious is the palace, so unused are many of its rooms, that it was a decade before anyone noticed her presence. When she was eventually discovered by the palace security they tried to evict her, but she protested that she had lived there for 10 years and it was her home.

— *Question 3* Is it her home?

You could use this question as an opportunity to explore the law surrounding 'adverse possession'. The UK law states that if a person occupies a portion of land without permission from the legal owner and remains there unopposed for at least 10 years, the land may become theirs. A notable of example of this was the case of Harry Hallowes who in 2007 acquired a small portion of Hampstead Heath having squatted there since the 1980s.

Are these laws fair? Are they reasonable? Or should land ownership be sacrosanct and inviolable?

Action 4 Describe the basic aspects of a nomadic way of life, perhaps focusing on a particular tribe or people such as the Nenets of Siberia.

— *Question* 4 Are nomads homeless?

- Do nomads have one home, many homes or no home?
- How long do you have to reside somewhere before it becomes a home?
- Is a hotel room a temporary home?
- Is a taxi a temporary home?

Action 5 Present the following argument –

1. Home is where you live.

2. You live in your body.

3. Therefore, your body is your home.

— *Question* 5 Is this correct?

- Are you inside your body?
- Is your body where you live?
- Is your body where you belong?
- Is your body a private or public space?
- Is your body a piece of land?
- The Book of Wisdom (9:15) describes the body as an 'earthly tent' – is your body temporary accommodation?

SELF

Topic Socrates advocated the ancient injunction, 'Know thyself'. For some, this session's questions will support that Socratic quest. For others, the baffled, they will subvert it.

Props Any book

Action **1** Ask the class to do as follows: Point to your toes. Point to your nose. Point to yourself.

— *Question* **1** Why did you point to where you pointed?

- — If I look you in the eyes, am I looking at *you*?
- — If I look you in the ears, am I looking at *you*?
- — For those who pointed to their entire body: imagine one of your toes got chopped off, which would be you? The toe or the rest?

> You could explore these questions through the story of Rapunzel. The prince first fell in love before he had even seen her. Though she was locked away in a tower, her singing voice filled the forest below and captured his heart. These feelings intensified when he saw the braids of her long golden hair flowing down from the high window.
>
> In relation to this story you could ask: In the beginning, had the prince fallen in love with Rapunzel or only her voice? (Is Rapunzel her voice?) Had he fallen in love with Rapunzel or her hair? While standing at the foot of the tower looking at her hair, was the prince looking at Rapunzel? If so, would he still be looking at her if he had snipped a piece off and taken it home to admire? While holding it, would he be holding her?

Action 2 Present a book to the class and ask how many things it is: Is it one thing or many things? One book or many sheets of paper? One story or many thousands of words? Then ask a volunteer (*x*) to stand before the class.

— *Question* 2 How many things is *x*?

- Is *x* one thing or many things?
- Is *x* made of many things?
- If *x* is only one thing, would it be possible to turn her into many things?
- If *x* is many things, by subtraction what is the least amount of things she could be?

Action 3 Tell the class the story of Mr and Mrs Oscitant. They both suffered from a condition which left them feeling constantly tired and low on energy. Every action required a huge amount of effort. For them climbing the stairs was a monumental undertaking which necessitated packed sandwiches and frequent breaks. They were hopeless at opening jars and by the time they'd finished buttering their toast it was always cold.

After years of marriage Mr and Mrs Oscitant decided they wanted a child, however, the time and energy required to look after and raise one was daunting, and possibly beyond their capabilities. They reasoned that though a whole child may be too much work for them, they might manage with half a child. But what is half a child? Is there such a thing? How might one be obtained?

Mr and Mrs Oscitant endeavoured to answer these questions, but it was hopeless. The questions were far too puzzling and arduous. After no more than five minutes of devilish thought the couple were left gasping and wheezing in a pool of their own sweat.

— *Question* 3 Is there a way to make half a child?

- Is there such a thing as half a person?
- Can people be halved like beds and tables?

— Are there any physical things that cannot be halved?
— If we are not physical things, what are we?

> To explore the implications of these subsidiary questions, present this argument and ask whether it is correct:
>
> 1. Physical things such as tables and chairs can be halved.
>
> 2. People cannot be halved – there is no such thing as half a person.
>
> 3. Therefore, people are not physical things.

Action 4 Present this argument to the class –

1. You were once an embryo.

2. Embryos do not have minds; they do not think.

3. Therefore, you and your mind are different things.

— *Question* 4 Is this correct?

Action 5 Present this argument to the class –

1. When a person dies, they stop existing.

2. When a person dies their body does not stop existing.

3. Therefore, a person and their body are different things.

— *Question* 5 Is this correct?

— If both arguments are correct and you are neither your mind nor your body, what are you?

TIME

Topic Though we are often preoccupied with how much or how little we have of it, we are less inclined to ask what it is. Yet over the centuries philosophers have spent a lot of time trying to understand exactly what it is they are spending, and in the process they've developed a variety of different theories on time's nature and being.

Presentism, for instance, is the view that neither yesterday nor tomorrow exist: only *now* exists. Eternalism, on the other hand, claims that the past, present and future do exist. Then there's substantivalism, the theory that time exists as an absolute entity independent of the events that occur within it, such that if everything were to freeze – the planets paused in their orbits, swallows motionless in their migration – time should nevertheless continue to flow.

Props A photograph

Action **1** Begin by simply asking 'What is time?' This usually generates many different ideas. You can focus your students' thinking by asking, 'Can you see it?', 'Can you feel it?', or the question below:

— *Question* **1** Was time invented or discovered?

   — If it was invented, could it have been invented differently?
   — If it was invented, can it be disposed of?
   — If it was discovered, how was it discovered?
   — Is it possible to live without being
     aware of the existence of time?
   — Can everything be classified as either
     invented or discovered?

Action 2 Show the class a photograph of anything you wish, from the berthed Titanic to your new cat.

> — *Question* 2 When you look at the photograph are you looking at the past?

Action 3 Present either or both of these arguments to the class —

The past is in the photograph, and the photograph is in the present, therefore the past is in the present.

My memories exist now, and the past is in my memories, therefore the past exists now.

> — *Question* 3 Is this correct?

Action 4 Present the following argument to the class —

1. The past no longer exists.

2. You cannot have what does not exist.

3. Therefore, you have no past.

> — *Question* 4 Is this correct?
>
> > — Does yesterday still exist?
> > — If the past does exist, where is it?
> > — If you made a promise yesterday, and yesterday no longer exists, does that mean the promise no longer exists?
> > — If yesterday you wrote a novel, but yesterday no longer exists, does that mean you are not its author?

- If the past exists in our memories, would universal amnesia erase the past?
- Does the past exist in its effects? Does yesterday's storm exist as today's floods?

Action **5** Present the following argument to the class –

1. The future does not yet exist.

2. You cannot have what does not exist.

3. Therefore, you have no future.

- *Question* **5** Is this correct?

  - Does tomorrow exist?
  - If the future does exist, where is it?
  - If the future doesn't exist, does this mean that a being like God who knew everything would not know what will happen to tomorrow?
  - Where does the future come from?

One of the benefits of using the above format to present arguments is that it makes the different components of the argument clear. Explain to the class that if they disagree with the conclusion, then they must disagree with either premise1 or premise 2.

If you think your class may struggle with this format, you can alternatively present the arguments to them as sentences e.g. 'Since the past no longer exists, and you cannot have what does not exist, it follows that you have no past'.

HUMANS

Topic It is alleged that humans were defined by Plato as featherless bipeds, only for his impudent contemporary Diogenes to interrupt one of his lectures swinging a plucked chicken and yelling, 'Behold, I have brought you a man.' Indifferent to the scowls from Plato's students, he then took a bite out of the uncooked bird (he would later die from eating raw octopus) and proclaimed, 'Diogenes the cannibal!'

The anecdote illustrates how Plato's attempt to provide an essential formulation of what a human being is (just as H_2O is the essential formulation of what water is) was undermined by a counterexample. Diogenes showed that Plato's definition was inadequate because not *all* featherless bipeds are humans.

This lesson challenges the class to succeed where Plato failed.

Props Cannibal Act template (see next page)

Cannibal Act 2020

An Act to make new provision about cannibalism, its prevention and the protection of .... from being killed and eaten.

[25th May 2020]

BE IT ENACTED by the Queen's most Excellent Majesty, by and with the advice and consent of the Lords Spiritual and Temporal, and Commons, in this present Parliament assembled, and by the authority of the same, as follows:—

Part 1

CANNIBALISTIC OFFENCES

(1) It is an offence to kill and eat all ....

Action Ask the class to imagine that cannibalism has become an increasingly severe problem in our society with people being killed and eaten on a daily basis. Their task as the government is to design an act of parliament legally proscribing and harshly punishing such acts. The catch, however, is that, for rigour's sake, they are not permitted to use the word 'humans', 'people' or 'persons' in the act. They can only use the following sentence forms:

— 'Creatures that *x*' (e.g. 'creatures that floss')

— 'Creatures with *x*' (e.g. 'creatures with nationalities')

For any proposed definition, ask –

— *Question* **1** Is this true for *all* humans? Is it true for *only* humans?

— Is there an essential difference between human and non-human animals?

— *Question* **2** Is anyone more human than anyone else?

> As stated elsewhere, a question without a corresponding Action is serving as its own stimulus. As such, try to use its presentation to enhance its catalytic powers. Write the question on the board with large imposing lettering to make it seem urgent, almost as though the question were confused by itself.

Parts & Wholes

Topic This session involves one of philosophy's classic thought experiments, the Ship of Theseus. It concerns identity and the extent to which identity can survive change.

Props None

Action Tell the story of the ship of Theseus –

Every nine years 14 young men and women were sent from Athens to Crete in order to be devoured by the Minotaur, a monster half-man and half-bull. To end this periodic slaughter, Theseus resolved to kill the Minotaur and so set sail from Athens. With the help of Ariadne, the princess of Crete, Theseus successfully decapitated the beast and returned home where he was given a hero's welcome.

Many years later, after Theseus had died, a museum in Athens bought his old ship and exhibited it for all to see. A gleaming gold plaque was placed beneath the ship which read, 'Behold, here stands the very ship that the hero Theseus sailed upon to defeat the Minotaur'.

After many years, however, the ship became worn and the wooden planks started to erode. In order to preserve the ship, when one rotten plank fell out the museum replaced it with a brand new one. Eventually, after hundreds of years of this piecemeal process, all of the original planks had been replaced. Nevertheless, the museum did not alter the gleaming gold plaque, which still told visitors, 'Behold, here stands the very ship that the hero Theseus sailed upon to defeat the Minotaur'.

— *Question* Was the museum lying?

- If it is the ship that Theseus sailed upon to defeat the Minotaur, given that its parts have all been replaced, what makes it that same ship?
- If it is not the ship that Theseus sailed upon, when did it cease being that ship? When the first plank was replaced? Or the final one? When?

Just as you can challenge and probe the idea that the museum is lying by asking at what precise point the ship was no longer the one that Theseus sailed upon, you can challenge the idea that the museum isn't lying by giving the thought experiment a twist: if the old discarded parts were reassembled to their original form, which ship would be the one that Theseus sailed upon? Both of them? How can that be?

A more general way you can further explore your students' thoughts is by presenting a parallel scenario: The House of Theseus. Imagine that the house in which Theseus was born had been likewise turned into a museum and advertised as 'The house of Theseus's birth'. Over time, as the bricks eroded, they were replaced with new ones, till, after hundreds of years, none of the original bricks remained. In this situation would it still be accurate to still refer to it as 'The house of Theseus's birth'? Is this case any different to the case of the ship? If so, how?

SIZE

Topic This session touches on a variety of different philosophical issues under the rubric of size and quantity. The first two questions, for instance, address the nature of space. The French philosopher Henri Poincare argued that nothing changes when everything changes because space, and concomitantly size, is defined in terms of the relation between things: if Mount Everest were the only thing in existence, it would make no sense to refer to it as tall. Unlike Isaac Newton, Poincare didn't believe that space was a sort of substance which exists independently of matter. Rather, it is defined by the relationship between matter.

With regard to the last question, here are George Bernard Shaw's thoughts: 'What you yourself can suffer is the utmost that can be suffered on earth. If you starve to death you experience all the starvation that ever has been or ever can be. If ten thousand other women starve to death with you, their suffering is not increased by a single pang... Poverty and pain are not cumulative... If you can stand the suffering of one person you can fortify yourself with the reflection that the suffering of a million is no worse...'

Props None

Action **1** Ask the class to imagine that while they slept last night, everything in the universe became 1000x larger, from our belly buttons to the sun. In fact, the process didn't stop: right now, with every passing second, everything is growing 1000x larger.

> — *Question* **1a** If this were the case, would we know it?
>
>> — Would any experiments confirm that this was happening?

— *Question* **1b** If this were the case, would anything actually be changing?

  — If everything changes in the exactly the same way, is that the same as nothing changing?
  — If a change makes no difference, does that mean it is not really a change?

Action **2** Tell the class to imagine that the reverse spell was cast on us and we all started rapidly shrinking.

  — *Question* **2a** As smaller creatures, would we have smaller lives?

    — Do smaller creatures have smaller deaths?

  — *Question* **2b** Would shrunken paintings have less beauty than they once did?

Action **3** Present this sentence to the class –

Smaller creatures have smaller feet, so when they have a pain in their foot, their pain is smaller.

  — *Question* **3** Is this correct?

    — Does pain have size?
    — Does it have location?
    — If it has location, does that mean it also has size?

Action **4** Show two paintings (Bellini vs. Mantegna, for instance): one with a single person being crucified (*x*) and another with three people being crucified (*y*).

  — *Question* **4** Does painting *y* show more suffering than painting *x*?

- Does it show 3x as much suffering?
- Can pain be quantified?
- If you double the amount of food in a tasty meal, does that make it twice as tasty?

PATHOLOGY

Topic The French philosopher Michel Foucault argued that many of our notions of illness do not correspond to an objective or scientifically neutral understanding but rather reflect our own historically conditioned and socially constructed norms and ideals.

This lesson invites us to consider how and when we decide that someone has something wrong with them, that is to say, the point at which difference becomes disease.

Props None

Action 1 Tell the class about Odette. She has an unusual condition which makes her fart loudly whenever she sings (or vice versa, I forget which).

— *Question* 1 Is there something wrong with Odette?

- Does Odette have a disease?
- Should she take medicine to stop it?
- If everyone had this condition, would that mean there was nothing wrong with her?
- If everyone except her had this condition, would that mean there was something wrong with her?
- Is it up to Odette to decide whether there's something wrong with her?

Action 2 To continue down the path of flatulence, tell the class of the ancient farting philosopher Diogenes (there was actually a philosopher who saved a man's life by farting – we won't get into it here, but if you're curious look up the story of Crates and Metrocles). Unlike most of us, Diogenes was immune to feelings of embarrassment or shame.

He would freely urinate and defecate in public and was unabashed by nudity. He couldn't care less what other people thought of him.

— *Question* **2** Was there something wrong with Diogenes?

- Did Diogenes have a disease?
- If there was nothing wrong with him for not feeling embarrassment, does that mean there is something wrong with those of us who do?
- Is there a way to test or determine whether it is he or we who have the disease?
- Are feelings of shame and embarrassment good for us?

Action **3** Tell the class about Mani. Mani doesn't care about anything, he never has. Whenever someone asks him how he feels or what he wants, he simply answers, 'I don't mind'. Even when his house burnt down and he lost all of his possessions, including his pet newt, he didn't mind.

— *Question* **3** Is there something wrong with Mani?

- Does Mani have a disease?
- If there were medicine that could make him care, should he take it?
- If there were medicine that could make him care, should he be forced to take it?
- Is he able to understand what is best for him?
- Is it possible to suffer without realising we are suffering?

Action **4** Tell the class about Simon. Simon believes that carrots talk to him. In other respects his behaviour is normal, and his attitude towards other root vegetables is one of general indifference, nevertheless, he frequently engages in lengthy conversations with carrots, even whilst eating them.

— *Question* **4** Is there something wrong with Simon?

- — Does Simon have a disease?
- — Is Simon insane?
- — Should Simon take medicine to silence the carrots?
- — Is there something wrong with thinking
  there is something wrong with us?

MEDICINE

Topic A complementary lesson to **PATHOLOGY**.

Props An apple, say (for illustrative purposes)

Action **1** Tell the class that you have in your bag a kind of medicine which you always carry with you. It helps to cure a disease you were born with and which you have suffered from your entire life. Though some of its users become addicted – an addiction which carries serious health risks – you have no choice but to take it. Forgetting to do so leads to discomfort, pain and eventually death. Even neglecting to take it for several hours can cause aggression and irritability. As medicine, it is very effective and relieves your suffering instantly. And though it's not offered by the NHS it is readily available and largely inexpensive.

Time for the reveal: it's food.

— *Question* **1** Is food medicine?

- — Is hunger a disease?
- — Can diseases be normal?
- — Is every need a kind of sickness?

Action **2** Tell the story of the Lotus eaters from chapter 9 of Homer's *Odyssey* –

After ten years of fighting and bloodshed the Trojan War came to an end, and Odysseus, king of Ithaca, was finally free to sail home to his family. But while at sea a vicious storm blew him and his crew miles off course. For over a week they battled the wind and the waves before eventually finding sanctuary on a small island.

Though Odysseus was eager to return to sea once the storm had lifted, the island was known for its famous lotus juice, a rare delicacy his crewmen were eager to try.

These poor men had been desolated by the long years of war, the years of separation from their families, the attrition of violence, the aches and pains of homesickness. Odysseus couldn't bring himself to deny them this small pleasure, this minor mote of joy. He told them to return by sunset and off they went.

By evening, however, they had not returned. Carrying a torch to light the way, Odysseus went in search of his crew fearing the worst: murder, disease or capture. But after two hours of looking, Odysseus discovered that the enemy he feared was in fact their own happiness.

Scattered across a moon-lit meadow, he found his men lying, smiling, supine on the ground, their mouths sticky with juice.

'Get up!' he ordered.

'Who are you?' one of them mumbled.

'Up! We're wasting precious time. The storm may return.'

'We're not going anywhere.'

Odysseus was perplexed. 'Why?'

'We feel very nice.'

'What about your home?'

'What home?'

'Ithaca!'

'Never heard of it.'

'What about your families?'

'What's a families?'

Odysseus leaned in to get a closer look and saw that their eyes were glazed and empty.

'Please sir, I want some more,' said one tugging at Odysseus's ankle and pointing to his mouth.

Odysseus quickly grasped the situation. The lotus juice was host to a kind of chemical that erases the memories of those who drink it. Having supped on the stuff, his crewmen had forgotten their homes and families, everything. This is why they were so happy and content. By erasing their memoires the juice had erased the source of their sadness, the cause of their sickness. They had fallen out of time and found themselves beneath the stars, swaddled in the queem quilts of forgetfulness.

— *Question* **2** Is lotus juice medicine?

  — Have the crewmen been cured of their sadness?
  — Is sadness a disease?
  — Is nostalgia an illness?

> You could use this question as an opportunity to explore the history of nostalgia, which in the 17th century was regarded as a medical condition. Indeed, the term was originally coined in order to facilitate medical diagnosis. Soldiers were seen as particularly susceptible, with symptoms thought to include malnutrition, hallucinations and even cardiac arrest. Treatments ranged from the unpleasant – leeches – to the extreme – execution. And though nostalgia is no longer regarded as a medical problem, should it be?

Action **3** Explain the concept of the elixir of life, or 'pill of immortality', perhaps outlining a few historical details and attempts. For example: over 2000 years ago the Chinese became interested in alchemy. Their attempt to transmute base metals into gold was not in order to become rich but to acquire immortality. It was believed that by consuming gold one could thereby assimilate its incorruptibility.

In *Ts'an T'ung Ch'i*, an ancient alchemist text, Wei Po-Yang described the effects of ingesting gold: 'The gold dust, having entered the five internal organs, spreads foggily like wind-driven rain. Vaporizing and permeating it reaches the four limbs. Thereupon the complexion becomes rejuvenated, hoary hair regains its blackness, and new teeth grow where fallen ones used to be. If an old man, he will once more become a youth; if an old woman, she will regain her maidenhood. Such transformations make one immune from worldly miseries...'

— *Question* **3** Is the pill of immortality (if such a thing existed) medicine?

- Is mortality a disease?
- Is aging (senescence) a disease?
- Would you take the pill?

Now

Topic The Scottish philosopher Thomas Reid claimed that the present is a point in time without duration. To speak of the 'present hour' or the 'present year' is convenient but incorrect: the present has no length.

   Henri Bergson, however, believed that the present does have a duration which is determined by one's field of attention. So long as actions and events remain of immediate interest to us they remain in the present. He suggested that with a powerful enough attention to life, our entire conscious history could remain within the present.

Props A clock

Action **1** Write the following question on the board –

   – *Question* **1** Is the time at which you started reading this question still part of the present?

      – If no, how short would the sentence have
         to be for the answer to be yes?
      – If yes, how long would the sentence have
         to be for the answer to be no?
      – How long is the present?

Action **2** Tell the class that you are going to try to make this current moment last for as long as possible. Ask them to sit quietly and raise their hands when they believe the moment is over. When all (or most) of the hands are up, ask –

— *Question* **2** How long does a moment last?

- — Can moments vary in length for different people?
- — Could it make sense for someone to say that there whole life is just one moment?
- — Could it make sense for someone to say there are no moments?
- — Can you experience more than one moment at the same time?

Action **3** Give the class 5 seconds and tell them to try to fill it with as many moments as possible. Next reduce the time frame to 1 second.

— *Question* **3** How many moments can you fit into a second?

- — Are moments things we can make?
- — Are moments things we can destroy?
- — How can you tell when one moment ends and another begins?
- — Does there have to be a gap between successive moments in order for them to be distinct things? If so, does that mean there are moments between moments?
- — Are moments real?

TALENT

Topic The 19th century writer Thomas Carlyle wrote, 'Looking round on the noisy inanity of the world, words with little meaning, actions with little worth, one loves to reflect on the great Empire of Silence. The noble silent men, scattered here and there, each in his department; silently thinking, silently working; whom no Morning Newspaper makes mention of... I hope we English will long maintain our *grand talent pour le silence*.'

Carlyle's view that silence constitutes a kind of talent raises the question of whether deficiency can ever constitute a talent. Though the word 'talent' originally referred to a unit of weight, can we have a talent for what we lack? How do we determine the difference between an ability and an inability? And can we have a talent for that which seemingly requires no effort, for the varieties of inaction? Should we ever admire, for instance, a person's breathtaking capacity for confusion or their stunning powers of boredom?

Props None

Action Tell the class to imagine that they are the producers of a television talent contest. Every week they are inundated with applications from people wishing to be on the show. The first decision that they have to make is whether the ability the candidate claims to have actually constitutes a talent. Naturally, amid the usual talents, such as singing and gymnastics, there are the slightly more eccentric, such as yodelling and Morris dancing, and then beyond these, well...

In any order you wish, run through the following 'abilities' found among the applications.

Confusion   Sadness
Boredom   Dreaming
Fear   Curiosity
Anger   Desire
Laughter

— *Question* Should this applicant be accepted onto the show?

- — Is it a talent?
- — Is it an ability?
- — Is it a skill?
- — Is it something you can learn?
- — Are some people better at it than others?
- — Is it admirable?
- — Is it a deficiency?

CONTROL

Topic While the control of other people is regarded as tyranny, self-control is hailed as a virtue. Nevertheless, for the 19th century biologist Thomas Huxley, self-control is an illusion. He advocated a theory known as epiphenomenalism according to which we do not have conscious control over our bodies. Our bodies work independently of our will. They are simply machines reacting to stimuli. When we catch a ball, for instance, this is not something we choose to do. Our senses detect the oncoming object, which causes activity in our nervous system, which leads to a movement in our muscles. Only as an effect of this process do we experience the intention of catching the ball. Mental events, such as decisions and intentions, are simply the consequences of our bodily processes and never the cause of them.

Props None

Action 1 Without offering a reason ask the class to stand up and then sit back down again.

> — *Question* 1 Did I just control you?
>
>> — Did you choose to stand up and sit down?
>> — Is obedience a choice?
>> — Did you want to stand up and sit down?
>> — Do I have power over you?

Action 2 Ask for a volunteer who thinks they cannot be controlled. Tell them you are going to make them blink by clapping in front of their face. (This has never failed, but if it does, keep going till you find a volunteer on whom it does work.)

— *Question* **2** Did I control you?

- — By blinking when I want you to, are you obeying me?
- — What is controlling you: me or your body?
- — Are your eyelids a slave to my clapping?
- — Are your eyelids a slave to your instincts?
- — Can you control your instincts?
- — If you do not have control, does that mean you are not free?

Action **3** Inform the class that you're now going to control their minds – resistance is futile. Tell them that you're going to make them all think about a plate of green wobbly jelly. Tell them that even if they try not to think about green wobbly jelly, they have to have in their minds the very thing they are trying to reject, namely, *green wobbly jelly*. There's just no way of shutting out the thought of the greenness, and wobbliness, and jelliness.

— *Question* **3** Did I control your mind?

- — By controlling your mind am I taking possession of it?
- — Are there things it is impossible to make another person's mind do?
- — Is it possible that you are being controlled in ways you don't even realise?
- — If you do not have control over your mind, does that mean it is not free?

Action **4** Ask everyone to wave, then to clap, then to give a thumbs up. Then present this argument:

1. Everything that obeys you is your slave.

2. Your hands obey you.

3. Therefore, your hands are your slaves.

— *Question* **4** Is this correct?

FRIENDS

Topic In an interview in 1982 the French philosopher Michel Foucault recounted how one of his friendships had originated in unusual circumstances: 'I remember very well that when I met the filmmaker Daniel Schmidt who visited me, I don't know for what purpose, we discovered after a few minutes that we really had nothing to say to each other. So we stayed together from about three o'clock in the afternoon to midnight... And I don't think we spoke more than twenty minutes during those ten hours. From that moment a rather long friendship started.'

If conversation isn't required for friendship, what is? At what point, and on what basis, does a person cease to be a stranger and become a friend? Or are the two categories – friend and stranger – not in fact mutually exclusive?

This lesson considers these questions in relation to the sad tale of lonesome Ron.

Props None

Action Tell this story –

> Ronald was a lonesome man. Every day he woke up alone, ate alone and watched television alone. As part of his daily routine he would also walk through the park, alone.
>
> One day while on his walk he sat down on a bench to rest. To his surprise he noticed there was a man sitting beside him with a bucket over his head.
>
> 'Hello', said Ronald. 'Why do you have a bucket over your head?'

The man was unresponsive.

'I suppose I can understand it,' Ronald said after a minute or so. 'Sometimes I'd like to hide under a bucket.' Ronald chuckled at the thought. 'Yes, I understand it very well,' he said.

He sat for a few more moments enjoying the silence before saying goodbye and walking home.

The next day he was pleased to find the man there again, despite the wind and rain. Ronald sat beside him.

'Hello again,' he said.

The man was motionless.

'Miserable day, isn't it?', Ronald commented. 'Weather like this can make me feel quite blue. Mind you, I often feel that way.'

Ronald turned to the man. 'You know, you're very easy to talk to,' he said. 'I haven't spoken this much to anyone in years.'

The man didn't reply.

When Ronald returned the next day the man was still there, and once again Ronald sat beside him and chatted.

This continued for several months till one day Ronald was saddened to find that the bench was empty. He sat down and looked around. There was no sign of the man. Ronald stayed there till sunset hoping he would return, but he didn't.

The following day Ronald again found that the bench was empty and, like the day before, he waited there till sunset, just hoping.

This continued for a few more days. Ronald started to worry. He decided to report the man's disappearance to the police.

At the police station Ronald explained that his friend had been missing for several days. The police asked for his friend's name: Ronald didn't know it. They asked for a description of his face: Ronald couldn't offer one. They asked for his age and ethnicity: Ronald had no idea.

The police soon lost their patience. 'You don't know anything about this man.'

'He's my friend,' Ronald replied.

'He's not your friend. He's a total stranger,' they said.

'We sit together.'

'I'm sorry, sir. Unless you can give us some concrete information about this individual, we can't help you.'

'I understand,' Ronald murmured, and walked home, alone.

— *Question* Was the man Ronald's friend?

- Is it possible to be friends with a stranger?
- Is it possible to be friends with someone you don't know?
- If he was a friend, was he a good or a bad friend?
- Can we be mistaken about who our friends are?
- Can you be friends with someone who isn't friends with you?
- Was Ronald the man's friend?

BONUS BEANS

QUESTION INVENTION

If you'd like your class to generate their own questions for discussion, you could ask them to use the following –

Combine the question structures with the words below to generate philosophical questions that perplex and intrigue you.

Can you *w y*?

Is *y z*?

Does *y x*?

w			
	Control	Divide	Consume
	Create	Break	Freeze
	Annihilate	Smell	Sell
	Touch	Feel	Buy
	Shrink	Own	Enslave
	Enlarge	Possess	Become
	Escape	Lose	See

x			
	Have a reason	Change	Decay
	Exist	Grow	

y

Time
Freedom
My mind
My body
Light
Reality
Dreams
Shadows
Thinking
The future
The past
Music
Sound
Art
Voice
Smells
Motion
Gravity
Property

Knowledge
Intelligence
Wisdom
Friends
Beauty
Love
Happiness
Education
The soul
Life
Thoughts
Sadness
Truth
Pain
Pleasure
Power
Silence
Darkness
Colour

Language
Words
Death
Chaos
Murder
Insanity
Humans
Animals
Confusion
God
Slavery
Nature
The universe
Authority
The wind
Existence
War
Peace

z

Real
An object
Infinite
Alive
Wrong
Beautiful

An illusion
Invisible
Everywhere
Nowhere
Useful
Good

Inside me
Powerless

PHILOSOPHICAL WRITING

Though essays are the standard academic form for philosophical writing, they are not necessarily the most conducive to philosophical thinking. Letter writing is an alternative I've sometimes employed.

Since letters have no standard structure and can be as meandering as conversations, they give students a form of exploring their thoughts without the distraction of structure and expectation. It could well be that you use this more free-associative format as a preliminary to essay writing.

I tell my students to imagine that they are writing to a person on the moon (or even the moon itself). By addressing the extraterrestrial they are given the tacit freedom to be as strange and alien as their recipient. In other words, by writing to the moon, they are vicariously adopting the cosmic stance of a moon-being, and this can help unfetter their thinking.

Generally, I give the class a specific question to focus on, an exemplar that they can use as a guide, and a suggested outline of what to include. For instance –

Dear Lunar,

Me again. Your favourite earthling. Here's the deal: tonight I am not writing to you from my bedroom but the bath... with my clothes on. You may ask why, but Lunar, you don't even know what water is, so how could I explain it to you? I'll try. It's like this: I realised that I could wash my clothes and myself at the same time by taking a bath while dressed. I have abolished the need for washing machines! Yes, Lunar, I know, I am a genius.

Also, like Archimedes, all my ideas come to me in the bath, and right now I'm wrestling with the question of whether it's ever OK to steal. For example, is it wrong to steal money from a rich person who will never realise it's missing? And is it wrong to steal if we're in need, like a poor hungry person who steals a sandwich?

Deontologists would say that if it's wrong in one case, it's wrong in all cases. They think that consequences don't matter. But I'm not sure about this – what's more important, a person's life or another person's property? I think life is always more important than property. And even if someone said property is more important, is my life not my property? By stealing, isn't the hungry person protecting her property?

What about the case where you steal something you don't need but no one notices? Well, there are no bad consequences, so how could it be wrong? I think I might be a consequentialist. They think that whether something is wrong or right is determined by its consequences. If the rich man never notices, no harm has been done, right? Or perhaps that is a disrespectful way of thinking. And maybe I should think about how it would affect him if he did find out. He wouldn't like it, I suppose. Maybe we shouldn't think about actual consequences but potential consequences.

But you know something I've just realised, Lunar? I'm thinking through these ethical questions but I'm making a metaphysical presupposition: I'm presupposing that there is such a thing as ownership and property! I mean, if no one owns anything, then there is no such thing as theft! Oh my oh my... I LIKE THIS IDEA!!! But does anyone own anything? How can I find the answer? Maybe by thinking about it some more. But not tonight. It's late and I need to shampoo my socks.

Buonanotte,

Z.

Task

- Like Z you are going to write a letter to a person on the moon, Lunar. You're going to use your letter as a way of exploring the philosophical question: ....

- You can imagine Lunar in any way you wish. All we know for sure is that he/ she lives on the moon. He/ She may even be the moon.

- In your first paragraph, start with a general introduction to Lunar. You might describe the kind of day you've had, what the weather is like, or other thoughts that are running through your mind. Be as playful or as serious as you want.

- For the rest of the letter start exploring your thoughts on the question:

  - Consider a reason why someone might answer yes to the question.
  - Consider a reason why someone might answer no to the question.
  - Try to work out what you think and why.

- End the letter with a farewell and anything else you may wish to add.

In the land of infinite time, one lovely way to mark their work is by writing them a return letter from Lunar. You can use the letter to ask questions about the things they've said and show them the implications and potential of their ideas.

ARGUMENTS

Here we have a few outcasts and oddballs, little arguments that didn't quite belong in any particular lessons. Nevertheless, these misfits can serve as the focal points of their own wee discussions.

Simply present one to the class and ask whether everyone agrees with the conclusion. If they don't, if the conclusion doesn't hold, given that it rests upon the foundation of the premises (and the reasoning that binds them together) the fault must lie with them, or with the reasoning. So which is it? Which premise is faulty? Or is there something fishy about the reasoning?

1. It is impossible to create nothingness.

2. Nothingness exists.

3. Therefore, it is impossible that God created everything.

1. The purest things are those that can never become dirty.

2. Dirt cannot become dirty.

3. Therefore, dirt is the purest thing.

1. If x is dependent on y, then x is no stronger than y.

2. We are dependent on air.

3. Therefore, we are no stronger than air.

Inspired by the ancient Greek philosopher Hipparchia –

1. Everyone is equal.

2. If everyone is equal, then an act which is permissible for one person is permissible for all people.

3. It is permissible for the Queen to slap the Queen.

4. Therefore, it is permissible for all people to slap the Queen.

1. We should only worry about things that can harm us.

2. Potential fires cannot harm us (my room is filled with potential fires, none of which are doing any damage).

3. Therefore, we should not worry about potential fires.

1. Snow White does not exist.

2. Only existent things have hair.

3. Therefore, Snow White has no hair.

1. If there is no law stating that we must do a certain thing, then we are free not to do it.

2. There is no law stating that we must follow the law.

3. Therefore, we are free not to follow the law.

Action Draw a diagram of the earth with a hole starting on one side in London and going right through so that it nearly comes out of the other side in Sydney. Draw a ball at the bottom of the hole –

1. The hole is in London.

2. The ball is in the hole.

3. Therefore, the ball is in London.

HOMEWORK PROJECT

I developed this for my students during the coronavirus lockdown, but it can also be used more generally as a homework project. The project, entitled *Journey to Earth*, invites students to imagine themselves as aliens exploring earth for the first time.

In many ways the philosopher experiences herself as an alien (or in the words of David Hume, a 'strange uncouth monster') as someone whose mad compulsion to think estranges her from common sense and shared belief. There is, therefore, a degree to which this project can serve as a primer or complement to your students' broader philosophical investigations.

I'll outline the structure and various prompts. Feel free to tinker and adapt. The preamble –

You're about to embark on a journey to a distant galaxy where you will visit a small and unassuming planet named earth. We know that there is life on earth. We just don't know what it is like. Your mission is to explore this foreign planet and record your findings. This will be our first contact with these alien life-forms so we are eager for your observations. We want to understand how they live and behave. We want an insight into their minds, their bodies and their actions. You may only have the opportunity to explore a house, or garden, or street – that's good enough. At this stage we only need a small sample size.

(a) Preliminary Stage

Experiments in alien thinking –

This project will require you to look at your familiar surroundings in a new way. The aim is to try to see it as though you were seeing it for the first time, as though you came from outer space. To help you mentally prepare for this strange exploration of your environment, work through the experiments and exercises below.

Choose at least five of these. After conducting an experiment, note down your findings.

1. **Look down at the sky:** Lie on the ground and imagine that the sky is beneath you. Imagine that your body is stuck to the ground and that you are looking down at the passing clouds and endless blue. (The indoor version: lie on the floor and look down at the ceiling.)

2. **Up and down:** In your head try to count up to 10 and down from 10 at the same time.

3. **Touch and Touched:** With the fingers of one hand stroke the palm of the other. Try to notice the two separate sensations of touching and being touched. What do you feel? One sensation or two?

4. **Become invisible:** Invisibility is easy to achieve. It only requires darkness. To fully experience your invisibility, find a very dark place, a cupboard for instance (you may need to do this at night). Climb into the dark place and take a hand-mirror with you. Hold the mirror up to your face and look at the blackness before you. Keep looking until you start to feel that you are looking at yourself, that you have become the darkness.

5. **Enter the mirror:** Look at yourself in the mirror and imagine that you are the reflection. You are the one inside the mirror. The real you is on the other side looking at you.

6. **Stand over an abyss:** Imagine that your household is suspended over a massive abyss. Just beneath the floorboards is a bottom-

less chasm, and as you walk across the floor, though you can't see it, this chasm is right there beneath your feet.

7. **Reverse time:** Imagine that time as we experience it is actually flowing backwards. The way reality really works is that life begins with our old decayed bodies waking up and gradually getting 'younger' till we eventually disappear into the womb. In reality, Shakespeare exists in the future and tomorrow exists in the past. But time has been reversed and everything is going backwards.
   Try to see the world this way while having a meal with your family. Though it looks as though the food is entering their mouths, this is a reversal of what is really happening. In the true flow of time food rises out of our bellies and emerges from our mouths.

8. **Puppet master:** Watch another person absorbed in their own activities. Imagine that you are controlling them. Their every action is something you are making them do.

9. **Forget how to read:** It's easy enough to make a spoken word lose its meaning; simply repeat it over and over (have a go). But it's harder to make a printed word lose its meaning. Find a word printed in a book, or magazine, or on food packaging, and keep looking until it becomes a meaningless sequence of disconnected shapes.

10. **Living hands**: Hold up your hand and wriggle your fingers. Imagine that the hand isn't being controlled by you but is an independent creature moving on its own accord.

11. **Pet humans:** Look out of the window. Try to spot someone walking their dog, but imagine that it is the dog walking the human.

12. **Impossibly gentle:** Using your index finger try to touch your wrist so gently you cannot feel it.

13. **Decapitate yourself:** With one hand under your chin and the other on top of your head, close your eyes and imagine you are holding your own decapitated head.

14. **Shrink and grow:** Imagine you and the room you are in have shrunk so that you are now only 5cm tall. Everything beyond your room and beyond what you can see is normal sized, but you are tiny.
Now try the opposite: imagine you are the size of a skyscraper. Everything beyond what you can see is the same size it always was, but everything within your field of vision is now massive. Your foot, for instance, is the size of your neighbour's house. Now imagine slowly alternating between these two states.

15. **Russian dolls:** Imagine there's another body inside your body, a person inside you, with arms inside your arms, and legs inside your legs, and a face beneath your face.

16. **Double vision:** Imagine there is another person looking out through your eyes seeing everything you see.

17. **Flatten the world:** This experiment can be done inside or out. Just sit and look straight ahead. Try to imagine that scene before you is flat. Imagine that it is 2-dimensional, like a painting. Though it may look as though there is depth, there is none. Depth is an illusion.

18. **All the world's a stage:** Imagine that everyone except for you is an actor. Everything they say is scripted. It's all a play. It's all pretend.

19. **Experience absence:** Think of all the strawberries in the world that aren't in your mouth. Your mouth is teeming with their absence. Can you feel this? Can you feel the absence of these strawberries on your tongue? Can you taste their absence? Look beside you. Can you see the absence of a rhinoceros? Can feel you the absence of a tail at the base of your back?

20. **Dream while awake:** Dreams are the effortless free-flowing stuff of the uninterrupted mind. We don't make dreams, we have them. They are experiences that happen to us when we relax our control of the mind and let it do its own thing.

    Try to achieve this effortless state of imaginative freedom while awake. Close your eyes and imagine a sycamore seed spinning towards the ground from a great height. From this image let your mind wander, not guiding it in any particular direction, but allowing any manner of strange image to arise and evolve. Try to have a waking dream.

For at least five of these exercises students are asked to record the results i.e. to answer the following questions:

Could you do it? Yes / No.

- If you couldn't do it, say why you think this was.
- If you could do it, describe what it was like.

(b) Homo sapiens

Students are asked to investigate three behavioural oddities of Homo sapiens. This involves describing the quirks, documenting why the earthlings think they do them, and then offering their own analyses and understanding of these behaviours –

Now you've landed, it's time to explore your foreign surroundings. Let's start with the alien inhabitants. To help you blend in we've given you the body of the most populous and seemingly dominant species, known as Homo sapiens. They'll be your first object of study.

By observing the aliens we've housed you with, try to notice three things they do which you find genuinely puzzling. This might be something as ordinary as watching TV or laughing or sleeping or singing or crying or talking or raising their voices or smiling. Or it might be specific to the individual you're observing, a curious habit, like biting one's nails. Perhaps it's something the aliens do together, like eating opposite each other on a raised surface they call a table, or dancing, or pretending to gun each other down in video games.

Ask the aliens themselves why they do it, then conduct your own analysis and arrive at your own conclusions as to why you think they do it (after all, they may not fully understand why they do the things they do).

(c) Gender

Students are asked to describe two gender differences they've observed and, as above, document the earthlings' explanations, as well as their own analyses –

Intelligence gathered indicates that Homo sapiens often divide themselves into separate genders. This is shown through their presentation and behaviour. For instance, those known as 'female' are more likely to have longer hair than those called 'male'. The 'females' are also more likely to paint their faces every morning, and the 'males' are more likely to hang bits of fabric around their necks (we understand these are called 'ties').

Please observe and analyse any gender differences you notice among the earthlings in your household.

(d) Your new alien body

This is possibly the strangest part of your journey. We have replaced your normal body, the body you've had your entire life, with a human body. This is to help you fully experience how these aliens experience the world. Please take the opportunity to explore your new incarnation, and please enlighten us on the following:

Nose: Our intelligence indicates that humans are able to experience things called 'smells'.

- — What are smells?
- — Do smells have smells? Yes /No.
- — Please describe the smell of your own nostrils.
- — Can you still smell while underwater? Yes / No.

Breathing: We understand that humans require oxygen to survive.

- — Are you always aware that you're breathing? Yes / No.
- — Is breathing a conscious act? Do you have to think about it? Yes / No.
- — Can you breathe through your nose and your mouth at the same time? Yes / No.
- — Can you breathe in and out at the same time? Yes / No.
- — How long can you go without breathing?

Voice: Humans apparently possess something called a voice.

- — How many voices do you have?
- — Can you make your voice come out of your nose? Yes / No.
- — Do your thoughts have a voice? Yes / No.
- — Can your thoughts be made louder and quieter? Yes / No.
- — If you put your hand in front of your mouth while saying 'Pretty penguins', can you feel your voice? Yes / No.
- — Can you make a sound that is larger than your body? Yes / No.
- — Can you make a sound that is so quiet only you can hear it? Yes / No.

Other: We have a few final questions we haven't been able to work out. You may need to do some research or ask the earthlings in your search for answers.

- What are lips for?
- Why do you have two nostrils instead of one?
- Why do bottoms stick out?
- Why do you have a line of hair above your eyes?
- Why aren't nails the whole length of your fingers?
- Why can't you sleep with your eyes open?
- Do you always fall asleep looking at your eyelids?

Overall:

- What is the most impressive thing about this alien body?
- What is the strangest thing about this alien body?
- Should we choose to bioengineer the human species, please suggest three alterations that could be made to improve their bodies.

(e) Alien objects

Students are asked to search their household to look for curious objects. They are to sketch the objects, and again ask for an earthlings' explanation of their functionality, then offer their own analyses.

Explore your household. Investigate what artefacts Homo sapiens have manufactured for themselves. Since you are now blessed with a nose, choose a room and conduct an olfactory investigation: smell it all, the walls, the carpet, the windows, the underside of the tables, everything.

- *Which object has no scent?*

- *Which object has the strongest scent?*

- *Which object has the most pleasant scent?*

- *Which object has the foulest scent?*

Now search the household and look for items whose purpose you just don't understand e.g. mirrors hanging in various places (why do humans constantly want to see reflections?), or paintings (why do humans frame and hang arrangements of colour and shape?), or beds (why do they sleep on raised surfaces suspended above the floor?), or cutlery (why don't they use their hands, which are themselves such marvellous instruments?), or houseplants (why do they bring the outside in?), or pets (why do they live with dependent animals?), and so on.

Finally, search your household and take an inventory of the following :

— *Strangest object*

— *Ugliest object*

— *Most beautiful object*

— *Most ingenious object*

— *Stupidest object*

(f) Conclusion

Students are asked to offer an overview of their impressions of earth and its human inhabitants. They are asked to recommend a course of action regarding the future relationship with earth: ignore it, learn from it or conquer it.

ONLINE RESOURCES

Should you wish to research any of the topics further, these websites may prove useful –

- Stanford Encyclopaedia of Philosophy:
  https://plato.stanford.edu/

- Internet Encyclopaedia of Philosophy:
  https://www.iep.utm.edu/

Podcasts –

- Philosophy Bites:
  https://philosophybites.com/

- In Our Time:
  https://www.bbc.co.uk/programmes/boo6qykl

- History of Philosophy Without Any Gaps:
  https://historyofphilosophy.net/

AFTERTHOUGHTS

In the best of all possible worlds, going to school – if such things existed – would mean growing up. Adulthood would be the aspiration. There would, as such, be little concern with discipline, duty or respect, for the concomitant imposition of standards and expectations is not conducive to growing up; it only serves to embalm the servility and dependence of childhood. Indeed, if adulthood means freedom – freedom to choose, to act, to live as we wish – then the best way to allow children to become adults is by allowing them to be themselves. Maturation, that is to say, is not mimesis. Growing up is not a process of emulating adults but one of separating from them.

The irony, in other words, of coercing children to behave like adults is that they are thereby trapped in childhood. Every new generation is a mutation of the species, and since we cannot know what the adulthood of tomorrow will involve, no one is qualified to teach anyone else how to be an adult. With this in mind, I'd like to suggest that in this best of all possible worlds, the curriculum – if such things existed – would include philosophy.

The compatibility between teaching philosophy and growing up lies in the fact that teaching philosophy is effectively not teaching; there are no lessons to learn. Inviting students to think, as philosophy does, involves relinquishing control (for you as much as for them). And this point serves to clarify why we should not conflate philosophy with critical thinking.

It is sometimes argued that students should be equipped with the skills to evaluate arguments, identify fallacies and recognise spurious assertions. Particularly in a world where we are always online and subject to the internet's wellspring of lies and misinformation, the ability to think clearly and critically is regarded as essential. Teaching philosophy is seen as the best way to impart these skills, yet this is neither true nor desirable.

If we want our students to listen to each other, to be open and curious, to learn the pleasures of influence, we should not teach them to erect boundaries of suspicion. Critical thinking adopts a stance akin to paranoia. It encourages an outlook whereby constant vigilance is required. It suggests deception, seduction even, is an ever-present danger. It is predicated on the assumption that everything we hear or read is guilty until proven innocent, that we must only absorb what we have already analysed. But this is not what education should be.

Imagine an RS lesson in which a student is emboldened to say she knows that God exists. She's asked how she knows this. 'Because I know he's watching over me,' she says. She's pressed on how she knows he's watching over her. 'Because fear never gets the better of me,' she answers.

Having apparently based a question of objective fact on her own subjective feelings, this student's comments do not withstand critical scrutiny. As such, those students versed in critical thinking might dismiss her remarks out of hand. Yet, whilst not bearing the certified hallmarks of reason, her comments may otherwise have had a profound effect on her peers. Far from being corruptive or toxic, her words may have been a great catalyst for their own thinking. She may have affected them in unfathomable ways.

We cannot know what will change us or how it will change us, and if education is supposed to be a process of formative change, then we should not teach our students to be dismissive of apparent nonsense. We should not pre-emptively impose limits on what they may find meaningful or enriching. And it is not even clear that such attempts to regulate thought are possible.

Thinking is bizarre. It is a power over which we have no power, something that we do yet that happens to us (it is perhaps more accurate not to say 'I am thinking' but 'Thought is happening to me'). This is not within the bounds of rules and norms. A child can no more think skilfully than she can grow skilfully. The effort to teach others how to think is as farcical and futile as Xerxes trying to whip the sea into submission.

None of this is to deny that thinking can descend into vapidity. It is certainly dispiriting to see students cling to beliefs with boorishness, belligerence or servility. We see education failing when we see students dismiss or accept ideas without consideration or interest. These failures, however, are not instances of bad thinking but of a lack of it.

Simplistically cast, thinking is letting thoughts happen, and thinking fails when the mind is not granted the freedom to let thoughts happen, when its fluidity is impeded. To encourage our students to think, we needn't burden their minds with additional skills, we simply need to remove the impediments of thought. These impediments, however, are considerable.

The disquieting reality of thinking is that it is intrinsically experimental, a plunge into the unknown. If we knew where our thoughts were going to take us, there would be no need to think in the first place. Without perplexity, puzzlement or confusion there is no thought, and so resistance to these states is resistance to thought itself. But these states are by their very nature unsettling, and so we are liable to defend against them by building armours of resentment and deference.

Where excessive deference stems from a fear of change and uncertainty – a fear of possibility – debilitating resentment arises from a fear of being conquered and overridden by alternative ideas and voices. In other words, whereas deference is wanting to be given the answer, resentment is wanting to hold onto it; both states are wedded to the cult of the answer.

To help students think we need to undo their fear of not knowing and their fear of being silenced. A pluralistic and non-hierarchical classroom can achieve this; a classroom, that is, in which students are accustomed to thoughts and ideas that are both ambiguous and abundant, where the supposed infallibility of authority and knowledge is looked upon as a strange fantasy.

The belief that there are sacrosanct and monolithic truths guarded by powerful authorities creates an insurmountable obstacle to thought. This understanding leads us to see truth as a zero sum game: the value of my belief depends upon the falsity of yours, and the value of your belief entails the worthlessness of mine. When I hear an alternative belief, I cannot bear to listen because it threatens to nullify my own belief. I must kill in order to survive. And if I cannot endure the fight, I will mindlessly defer, I'll escape the fray by surrendering. I will not speak, nor will I think, because I do not want to be wrong, and I am afraid of being attacked.

This environment, governed by a fight to be right, forecloses the possibility of thought. It doesn't give students the necessary space or freedom in which to be experimental in their thinking. An alternative environment, one conducive to thought, would be constituted by the belief that passionate opposition to an idea needn't require its annihilation. This alternative environment would be free from competition. It would be one in which students are not made to see themselves as either inferior or superior to each other. One in which they are not conditioned to think of their work in terms of grades and levels. It would not reward fast answers or domineering voices. It would rather celebrate the inconstancy of the mind, the fecundity of confusion, the impermanence of facts and the incompleteness of knowledge.

The student at home in this environment is best characterised not as a critical but a confident thinker. Confident thinkers have no need to defensively screen alternative beliefs because they desire new influences and delight in the unpredictability of their minds. Since they know there are no absolute authorities, they trust their own power to think. Feeling no obligation to obey, they have no reason to fight. Recognising that truth is not a zero sum game, they do not regard listening as a form of submission.

The confident thinker does not think with the certainty that she is right. She thinks without the fear of being wrong, or of appearing stupid, or of being ignored. This freedom from both resentment and deference is based on a trinity of vital attitudes: It is OK to change my mind. It is OK to be confused. It is OK to be different.

Critical thinking is both stifling and coercive, and by its imposition of norms it introduces new ways of getting it wrong, of being humiliated.

It also risks compromising the great redeeming feature of schools: the very fact of leaving home to be immersed in a vast body of different people with different lives and different thoughts. Schools should be organised so as to harness this opportunity, not to thwart it. They should encourage openness rather than suspicion. They should teach the pleasures of influence rather than the dangers of deception.

In order to cultivate this immersion and openness, we should jettison, along with the idea that philosophy is connected to critical thinking, the notion that philosophy is a forum for sharing. Given the fluidity of thought, while in the process of thinking there is nothing to share; belief and opinion are held in abeyance. To think is to exchange your bounded island for the open sea. A philosophy lesson, then, is not a space in which to exchange points of view but an opportunity for symbiosis. It is not, in other words, about sharing but intermingling. The class itself becomes a sort of thinking thing, a strange kind of entity, bound by knots of conflict and confusion, coruscating with sudden bursts of energy.

The quest, in essence, is not to reason but to think. Where reason is defined, bounded, prescriptive and coercive, thinking is shifting, boundless, exciting and feral. Reasoning keeps everything in its right place, but to think is to defy the forces of inhibition and resistance – a joyous feat. And if nothing is worthwhile without joy, then philosophy with children should endeavour to steer them away from the stifling strictures of reason and lead them headlong into the hurly-burly weathers of thought.

INDEX

OTHER TITLES PUBLISHED BY THE PHILOSOPHY MAN

These popular A6 minibooks by Jason Buckley are excellent compact guides to practising philosophy for children.

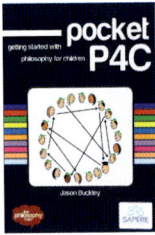

Pocket P4C explains the most common methods of P4C.

Thinkers' Games show how to make thinking physical to promote engagement.

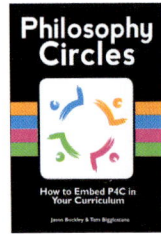

Philosophy Circles explains how to embed philosophy in your curriculum. Written with Tom Bigglestone.

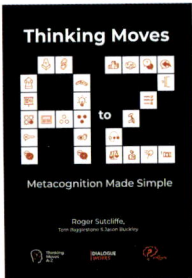

By Roger Sutcliffe with Jason Buckley and Tom Bigglestone, Thinking Moves A-Z: Metacognition Made Simple provides a practical language of 26 key moves, from thinking **Ahead** to **Zooming** in. It transforms metacognition from a nice idea in theory to an everyday part of learning and teaching.

For consultancy and training in schools, or to buy these titles, go to:

www.thephilosophyman.com

For live philosophy sessions on Zoom, go to: **www.p4he.org** or **www.giftcourses.co.uk**